International Management English

Leading People

Steve Flinders

DELTA Publishing
Quince Cottage
Hoe Lane
Peaslake
Surrey GU5 9SW
England

York Associates
Peasholme House
St Saviours Place
York YO1 7PJ
England

www.deltapublishing.co.uk

www.york-associates.co.uk

First published 2012

Edited by Catriona Watson-Brown
Designed by Caroline Johnston
Illustration on page 14 by Kathy Baxendale
Cover photo © Dreamstime
Images by Shutterstock (pages 8, 18, 28 (top), 29 (bottom), 35, 38 (bottom), 48 (bottom), 60 (bottom left)); Thinkstock (pages 10 (top), 15, 20 (both), 25 (both), 28 (bottom left), 38 (top), 40, 48 (top), 50 (both), 54, 58 (top), 70, 78 (both), 80); Jeremy Comfort (page 10 (bottom)); Cartoonstock (pages 17, 27, 32, 37, 60 (top), 63, 68 (top), 72, 77); iStock (pages 28 (bottom right), 29 (top), 58 (bottom), 60 (bottom right), 68 (bottom), 75, 84); Professor Beverly Alimo-Metcalfe (page 42); Pepijn Kramer www.flickr.com/photos/peregrin71 (page 45); David Gurteen (page 52); Christopher James (page 64); Joseph Nye (page 82)
Cover design by Clare Webber
Printed in Malta by Melita Press

ISBN Book 978-1-905085-67-5

Author acknowledgement

The author would like to thank Jeremy Comfort, whose ideas about developing people internationally underpin this book and without whom it would not have been possible.

Text acknowledgements

We are grateful to the following for permission to reproduce copyright material:
Mr Neil Atkinson, Deminos, for a quotation and material on pages 12 and 59, from www.deminos.co.uk Blog no. 16, 2 April 2011 and Blog No. 34, 20 August 2011, copyright © Deminos. Reproduced by kind permission; TMS Development International Ltd for extracts on pages 12–13, 16 and 18–19, from 'TMS set of linking skills' and 'Four TMP dimensions for establishing people's workplace preferences'. All content relating to Margerison-McCann Team Management Systems, including the Margerison-McCann Types of Work Model and the Margerison-McCann Linking Skills Model, are reproduced by the kind permission of TMS Development International Ltd, 2012. ® The Margerison-McCann Types of Work Model is a registered trademark; York Associates for extracts on pages 22–23, 53, 66, 78–81, 86, from *Developing People Internationally* model by Jeremy Comfort, York Associates 2007; *Some Golden Rules for Negotiating Successfully* by Bob Dignen, York Associates; *How to Learn Languages for International Business* by Steve Flinders, York Associates; exercises and activities from *Developing People Internationally* support materials Unit 7, Representing, 2008 by Jeremy Comfort and Bob Dignen. Reproduced by permission of York Associates, www.york-associates.co.uk; Guardian News & Media Ltd for extracts on pages 32–33 and 43, from 'Who's the boss?', *The Guardian*, 2 February 2011; and 'Why staff rate female leaders highly but male bosses score them lower than men' by Beverly Alimo-Metcalfe, *The Guardian*, 14 September 2011, copyright © Guardian News & Media Ltd 2011; Nicholas Brealey Publishing for an extract on page 34, adapted from 'Icebreaker – Draw a House' in *Developing Intercultural Awareness: A Cross-Cultural Training Handbook*, 2nd edition, by L. Robert Kohls and John M. Knight, 1994. Intercultural Press Inc. Reproduced with permission; Wikipedia for the extract on 'Interpolis' on page 45, Wikipedia, http://en.wikipedia.org/wiki/ Interpolis, granted under the GNU Free Documentation License (GFDL); The Random House Group Ltd for the book cover on page 47 from *Know-How: The Eight Skills That Separate People Who Perform From Those Who Don't* by Ram Charan, published by Random House Business Books. Reprinted by permission of The Random House Group Limited; David Gurteen for a photograph and extract on page 52, from 'We must stop doing things to people' by David Gurteen, *Inside Knowledge Magazine*, 5 March 2010, Volume 13, Issue 5, www.gurteen.com, copyright © David Gurteen. Reproduced by kind permission; Nigel Ewington for an extract on pages 54–55, from 'list of TIP (The International Profiler) competences and behaviours' by Nigel Ewington, Worldwork. Reproduced with kind permission; Brefi Group for an extract and table from page 62, adapted from 'Coaching and mentoring', http://www.brefigroup.co.uk/coaching/ coaching_and_ mentoring.html, source: CIPD. Reproduced by permission of Brefi Group; Mr Christopher James, Rexel for an extract and table on pages 64 and 72, from *Rexel Learning Site 30.2 Perception of Time* pp.96–97, and an extract and photograph from *Rexel Learning Site 22 Performance Gap Analysis*, pp.64–67 by Christopher James. Reproduced with kind permission; CAL Learning for the blog article on page 74, 'Giving Feedback across Cultures' by Lauren Supraner, 1 March 2010, http://www.callearning.com/blog/2010/03/ performance-feedback-across-cultures, copyright © CAL Learning; Joseph S. Nye, Jr for a photograph on page 82. Reproduced by kind permission; and Oxford University Press for an extract on page 82, from *Leadership: A Dozen Quick Take-Aways* by Joseph Nye Jr. 2008, pp.147–148. Reproduced by permission of Oxford University Press and the author Joseph S. Nye, Jr.

In some instances we have been unable to trace the owners of copyright material and we would appreciate any information that would enable us to do so.

Contents

Introduction

At York Associates, we always aim to develop the skills which help professionals to do their jobs better. In recent years, we have worked hard to enrich our Business English and professional communication training with intercultural content. More recently, we have included a focus on important interpersonal and management skills for listening, building relationships and trust, influencing, etc.

Our approach is built on the premise that good communication is vital to achieving results at work. Effective international communicators need a blend of language, professional communication, intercultural and management skills to be successful.

Welcome to *International Management English*, a new series published jointly by York Associates and Delta Publishing. The four titles in this series are:

- *Leading People*
- *Managing Projects*
- *Working Virtually*
- *Managing Change*

Each book includes either one or two audio CDs.

Professional language training with a management focus

Each book consists of eight units of study, containing four main sections per unit:

- *Section A: Discussion and listening*
  Engaging and relevant content in areas of international management and teamwork
- *Section B: Communication skills*
  Opportunities for the practice of key skills in areas such as conflict management, team building and giving/receiving feedback, as well as more familiar topics such as presentations, meetings, negotiations and writing e-mails
- *Section C: Professional skills*
  Authentic texts from leading management writers and thinkers, designed to encourage reflection and debate among readers
- *Section D: Intercultural competence and Case study*
  A focus on raising intercultural awareness, followed by illustrative case studies which are drawn from the authors' experience of the international business world

In addition, the book offers:

- a strong emphasis on vocabulary learning, with glossaries of key terms at the end of each unit
- practical tips on how to improve performance at work
- the opportunity to use a learning diary, which encourages the setting of realistic goals to implement the learning points from each unit.

At the end of the book, the Word list provides a useful list of key words, referenced to the page where the term is defined.

Having worked through the book, you will have developed not only your business language skills but also your ability to communicate and manage real challenges in your international working environment.

To the teacher

The four titles in this series represent a new development in ELT. They broaden the scope of teaching to include highly relevant management topics and skills. The materials are not only engaging for teachers, allowing them to introduce and develop new management communication skills in an ELT classroom; students are also motivated as they learn how to manage real professional communication challenges which they face at work on a daily basis.

Each title is designed primarily for work with both small and larger groups, but can also be used in one-to-one situations and has many features which will support self-study.

Across the eight units of each title, there is a strong focus on developing fluency and skills to communicate effectively in real work situations. There are opportunities to practise listening, reading and writing skills. The intercultural case studies in Section D are drawn from real-life examples and provide engaging discussion and problem-solving material for the ELT classroom.

There is online support for trainers (www.delta publishing.co.uk/resources) in the form of notes for each unit, which provide background information on the management topics and skills presented. There are also podcast interviews with the authors in which they discuss the ideas in the different titles, with practical tips for teachers on how to deal with the various topics and skills in the ELT classroom.

A final word

To both learner and teacher, we would like to express the hope that you find the materials stimulating, and that they help people to communicate more effectively at work.

Learning diary

Accelerate your learning by using this 'learning diary'. Make eight photocopies of this page, one for each unit. Note down important new words and expressions from the unit as you study. Make notes to help you remember any good advice you get on how to communicate and be effective across cultures. Then decide on some actions you can take to help to consolidate the things you have learned.

Unit number: _____

---

1 Language

Important (new) words and expressions for me from this unit are:

---

2 Professional communication skills

Important (new) expressions and communication tips for me from this unit are:

---

3 Intercultural competence

Important information/tips to be effective across cultures for me from this unit are:

---

4 Actions

To help me to consolidate all the learning points above, I need to:

Needs analysis

Introduction   You can use this Needs analysis to help you think about how to make the most of this course and to maximise your learning.

Your communication network   First, think about who you communicate with in English. Draw a communication network showing the individuals or groups of people with whom you communicate in your work. Follow the example and note down the medium of communication you use, e.g. face-to-face, phone, e-mail, teleconference, etc., for each of them.

customers

boss — team members

weekly team meetings, face to face, informal chats in corridor and during lunch, occasional evening social events. E-mail contact with team members in Brazil.

Think about your communication network. Have you got your priorities right? Have you got the type of communication right in each case? Are you spending the right amount of time communicating with each individual or group?

Your communication needs   What do you have to do in English? Think about your communication profile in English as you complete these tables. For frequency, use a scale of 1 to 5 (1 = never, 2 = occasionally, 3 = sometimes, 4 = often, 5 = very often). For difficulty, use another scale of 1 to 5 (1 = very easy, 2 = easy, 3 = sometimes causes problems, 4 = difficult, 5 = very difficult). Where are the biggest gaps?

Leadership skills

skill	frequency	difficulty
Building a team		
Giving direction		
Organising people		
Defining roles for people		
Providing support for people		
Giving and receiving feedback		
Representing the team		

Professional communication skills

skill	frequency	difficulty
Presenting		
Meeting		
Negotiating		
Telephoning		
Socialising		
E-mailing		

Interpersonal skills

skill	frequency	difficulty
Building relationships		
Networking		
Building trust		
Influencing		
Making decisions		
Managing conflict		

Your language and communication challenges

You lead people in an international context and you use a foreign language to do so. Think about and write down what the biggest language and communication challenges facing you are:

1 ....
2 ....
3 ....

Your intercultural challenges

What are the biggest intercultural challenges that you face?

1 ....
2 ....
3 ....

Your current learning objectives

What would most help you to improve your ability to communicate effectively in an international context? Think carefully about this question and then write down your answers.

1 ....
2 ....
3 ....

Your future learning targets

As part of your learning plan, what targets can you fix for yourself? Start a learning diary (see page 5) and set targets for your future learning using this frame:

In one month's time, I aim to be able to ....
In three months' time, I aim to be able to ....
In six months' time, I aim to be able to ....
In one year's time, I aim to be able to ....

Becoming a better manager

*True leadership must be for the benefit of the followers, not the enrichment
of the leaders. In combat, officers eat last.*

Robert Townsend (1920–1988),
CEO of Avis and author of *Up the Organisation*

AIMS

A To understand what makes a good manager
B To study effective communication techniques
C To reflect on the skills good managers have
D To learn some basic tools of intercultural communication

A Discussion and listening

Think about it

1 Who have you managed, and in what situations? Give your partner a brief summary of your management experience.

2 Which of these words and phrases do you associate with managing? Compare your answers with a partner.

boring
challenging
difficult
easy
exciting
rewarding
something you're born with
something you can learn

Marcus Aurelius, Roman emperor (161–180 AD) –
a great leader and a great leadership thinker

3 What do you think makes a good manager? Work with a partner to produce what you think are the eight most important qualities and skills of a good manager. Then compare your results with those of other pairs.

Listen to this

4 🎧 **1** Listen to an interview with Hélène Baron, Director of Human Resources in a large French company. She talks about becoming a manager.
  a What is Hélène's first definition of a manager?
  b What is her other definition?
  c Does she think we can teach people to manage?
  d What choice should we all be encouraged to make?

5 🎧 **2** Listen to the second part of the interview and answer these questions.
  a How did she feel when she first became a manager? Why?
  b What is MBWA?
  c What else did she learn?

6 Complete these sentences with the correct form of the word *manage*.

a She doesn't have a lot of experience but I'm sure that one day she'll make a good

....

b He's quite new to .... , so you would expect him to make a few mistakes at the beginning.

c He showed few .... qualities while he was in the post.

d Some of the people in that department can be so difficult that sometimes they are hardly ....

7 Complete each of these typical word combinations with the correct form of *manage* so that they match the definitions.

a .... buyout — when a company's managers buy the company they work for

b .... director — the top manager in a company

c marketing .... — the person in charge of marketing in a company

d .... fund — an insurance company investment fund for small investors

e middle .... — the organisational layer between junior and senior in a company

f .... board — the senior committee responsible for the day-to-day operations of a company

g .... experience — what you need to be a good manager

h micro-...................... — to direct and control people in a very detailed way

8 Match the verbs (1–10) with the words or phrases (a–j) to make a list of management qualities.

A good manager ...

1	has	a	clearly.
2	builds	b	objectives.
3	gets	c	mistakes and recognises this.
4	implements	d	roles clearly.
5	adds	e	shocks.
6	communicates	f	value.
7	makes	g	a vision.
8	sets	h	trust.
9	defines	i	strategy.
10	absorbs	j	results.

9 Describe a good manager you know. Try to use words and phrases from this section.

10 What is your management profile? Create a brief profile of yourself and present it to your partner.

Management experience before full-time employment:

Years of management experience:

Different management positions:

Number of people responsible for:

What I like about managing:

What I don't like about managing:

As a manager, what I'm good at:

Where I need to improve:

Think about it **1 Which of these do you spend most time doing in English?**

    a presenting
    b taking part in meetings
    c leading meetings
    d writing
    e telephoning
    f tele- and video-conferencing
    g business socialising
    h other

Which do you like most and least?
Share your answers with a partner.

Jeremy Comfort

Listen to this **2** 🎧 **3** **Jeremy Comfort is an expert in international communication. He helps managers all over the world to communicate more effectively at international level. Listen to him talking about the Four Ps of business communication.**

    a Note down what the Four Ps are.
    b Why does Jeremy think that people should spend more time thinking about communication?

3 🎧 **4** **Jeremy talks about the nine stages that different communication situations have in common. As you listen, write down each of the stages (a–i).**

Focus on language **4 You are planning an event and need to communicate with others about it. Complete the table on page 11, matching statements a–d to the Four Ps.**

    a Different people – especially ones from different cultures – may have different ideas about *how* the event should be managed. We mustn't take it for granted that the way we do things is the same as the way they do things. We need to agree on rules and procedures at the start.
    b Everyone needs to be clear about who does what. We need to know what contribution each of us is expected to make.
    c We have to think carefully about what needs to be done in advance in order to make the event a success.
    d We have to be clear about the aims of the event, and we have to make sure that everyone understands and accepts these. (If they don't, we may have to negotiate new ones.)

the Four Ps	statement
P.............¹ (= planning)	
P.............² (= objectives)	
P.............³ (= rules)	
P.............⁴ (= roles)	

5 **Match each of these statements (1–9) with one of the nine stages in the communication process (a–i), which you wrote down in Exercise 3.**

1 That concludes our business for today.

2 I propose that we adopt all three of Donald's suggestions.

3 It's very important to get this right, so I need to spend a lot of time thinking about it beforehand.

4 Does everyone agree that these are the three decisions that we've reached today?

5 I think that was a very successful outcome. Good work, everyone.

6 Welcome to this special event.

7 So here is the programme I propose to work through.

8 Can you deliver by the end of the month?

9 Have you been to Beijing before?

6 **Identify your own phrases for each of the stages in the communication process, then share them with the rest of the group.**

Let's talk 7 **Work in groups of three. Two of you (Students A and B) are going to discuss an employee problem, while the third person (Student C) observes the discussion and gives feedback afterwards.**

Student A: Turn to page 90.
Student B: Turn to page 95.
Student C: Turn to page 96.

Try to use some of the phrases from this section while you are doing the role-play.

8 **Look again at the list of communication contexts in Exercise 1. Choose one of them and discuss with a partner how you could improve communication in your organisation in that context, using the Four Ps and the communication processes you have learned about.**

Example:

Meetings
We could start each meeting by celebrating a recent achievement.

E-mails
We could all agree not to read any e-mails before midday.

C Professional skills: What good managers do

Think about it

1 Look at the Johari Window, named after its creators, Joseph Luft and Harry Ingham, then think about the questions below.

	known to self	unknown to self
known to others	my public self	my blind spots
unknown to others	my hidden self	my unconscious self

Johari Window

Self-understanding is an essential quality for managers. Good managers not only know themselves quite well, they also know how others see them.

The Johari Window is designed to encourage us to know ourselves better. It can also help improve mutual understanding of people within a group. In this diagram, the quadrants are of equal size, but in reality their relative size varies from individual to individual.

a My public self: How far does your picture of yourself match the picture that other people have of you? How do you know?

b My blind spots: How far are you aware of how others see you? Do you have ways of finding out how other people see you? What do you do?

c My hidden self: Would it help to build more positive relationships at work if colleagues knew more about you?

Discuss your ideas with others in the group.

Read this

2 Neil Atkinson set up Deminos, an HR and employment law firm, in London in 2007. He writes a regular blog for British managers. Read the extract on leadership and answer these questions.

a Why should many British managers recognise that they are seen as bad leaders?

b What are the two things that staff expect managers to do?

c What does Neil Atkinson mean by 'predictive management'?

d What does he say we should do to get better at predictive management?

Are we bad leaders?

More than half of our employees think so. According to a study by the Kenexa Research Institute, only 47 per cent of staff in the UK felt they had an effective leadership team. This number was lower than that recorded in India (69 per cent), Brazil (59 per cent), the US (54 per cent), China (53 per cent) and Canada (52 per cent), although only 33 per cent of employees in Japan rated their management as effective. It's good to know we're considered better than the Japanese managers, although ironic, given we were following Japanese management techniques such as total quality management and *kaizen* back in the '80s and early '90s. This means we are below the international average of 51 per cent. So are we bad managers?

Jack Wiley, Executive Director of Kenexa Research Institute, said: 'UK employees view their senior leadership team as effective if it:

- responds quickly to marketplace opportunities and competitive threats
- keeps them informed about organisational issues
- prioritises quality and improvement
- motivates people to work hard.'

It seems to me that if we listen to what our employees are telling us, they want us to make good decisions and communicate with them. And if we do these two things, our people might think we are half-way decent at our jobs. We've talked a bit about our communication, but what about decision-making? As a leader, and particularly if you are the ultimate leader, it's critical to keep looking forward – to predict potential issues and prepare for them before they happen. In this way, we can make good decisions. I call this 'predictive management'.

And to get better at predictive management, you need to start by scheduling a meeting with yourself each and every week. Block out half an hour of time, close the door, turn off your phone and think.

Identify the biggest headache for your business, then allow yourself to just think about it ... what caused it, what warning indicators were there, how did you fix it, what can you do to reduce the chances of it happening again?

Hey ... this sounds a bit like that Japanese Total Quality Management system, only better.

---

3 Discuss these questions.

a How good do you think you are at:
- responding quickly to marketplace opportunities and competitive threats?
- keeping people informed about organisational issues?
- prioritising quality and improvement?
- motivating people to work hard?

b How good do you think your organisation is in general at doing these things?

c Do you think that scheduling meetings with yourself is a good idea? Is it realistic for you? What is the biggest headache for your business that you would think about?

Focus on language **4** Look through the blog extract to find words/phrases which mean the same as these:

a assessed	**d** forecast	**g** reserve
b reacts	**e** problems	**h** problem
c top	**f** planning	**i** signs

5 Not all managers are leaders, and not all leaders are managers, but good managers and leaders often want to know more about both. Complete these sentences with *managers* or *leaders* as appropriate.

a .... lead people.   .... manage tasks.

b .... set a new direction or vision for a group that they follow.

.... control or direct people and resources in a group according to principles or values that have already been established.

c .... have subordinates.   .... have followers.

d .... are proactive.   .... are reactive.

e .... take risks.   .... minimise risks.

f .... make rules.   .... break rules.

g .... have formal authority.   .... do not need formal authority.

h .... think step by step.   .... think radically.

6 For each of the pairs of sentences in Exercise 5, how far would you say that you are more of a manager, or more of a leader? Discuss your answers with a partner.

Let's talk **7** Dr Charles Margerison and Dr Dick McCann, the developers of Margerison-McCann Team Management Systems, created a set of what they call 'Linking Skills'.
Linking Skills are necessary to integrate and co-ordinate the work of the team. Unless these skills are used well, the team will lose momentum and direction and team performance may suffer.
As a result of extensive interviews with teams and team leaders throughout the world, Margerison and McCann identified 13 key linking skills which fall into three areas (shown below).

> **PEOPLE LINKING SKILLS**
> **Active Listening** Listen before deciding.
> **Communication** Keep team members up to date on a regular basis.
> **Team Relationships** Encourage respect, understanding and trust amongst team members.
> **Problem Solving and Counselling** Are available and responsive to people's problems.
> **Participative Decision-Making** Involve team members in the problem solving of key issues.
> **Interface Management** Co-ordinate and represent team members.
>
> **TASK LINKING SKILLS**
> **Work Allocation** Allocate work to people based on their capabilities and preferences.
> **Team Development** Develop balance in their team.
> **Delegation** Delegate work when it is not essential to do it themselves.
> **Objectives Setting** Set achievable targets with the team, but always press them for improved performance.
> **Quality Standards** Set an example and agree high-quality work standards with the team.
>
> **LEADERSHIP LINKING SKILLS**
> **Motivation** Inspire others to give their best.
> **Strategy** Devise effective action plans to achieve goals.

If you would like to learn more about the Linking Skills, you can do so at www.tmsdi.com.

How far do your skills complement those of other people in your group? How far do they complement the skills of the people you work with?

D Intercultural competence: Some basic tools of intercultural communication

The way we do things round here

Culture as defined by Fons Trompenaars,
author of *Riding the Waves of Culture*

1 **Which of these words and phrases do you think are relevant to a discussion about cultural difference?**

attitudes to time   geography   hierarchy   history
McDonald's   music   politicians   sport

2 **We use the concept of the 'culture onion' to understand that we all have layers of culture, which have an impact on our thoughts and behaviour. What layers can be added to this onion? (See page 91 for other suggestions.)**

The culture onion

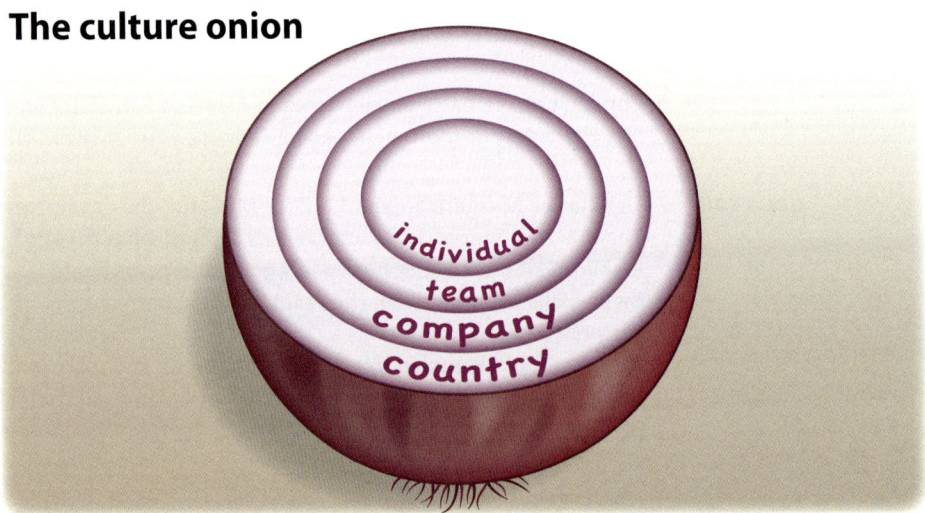

3 **What does your own 'culture onion' look like? Draw it, then explain it to a partner.**

Focus on language **4** **Complete the word combinations below with a word from the box to fit these statements about different aspects of culture.**

briefing	clash	corporate	functional	shock

a Every company has a different look and style.
.... **culture**

b Joe is going to live in Argentina for a year, so his company paid for him to do a course on living and working there.
cultural ....

c When Miguel and Dmitri started working together, there was a lot of misunderstanding and conflict at first. Their backgrounds are so different.
culture ....

d When Jim first arrived back in New York after spending a year in the Amazon jungle, he experienced a strong reaction to the unfamiliarity of his surroundings.
culture ....

e The culture of, for example, the scientists in our research centre is different from that of our marketing people.
.... **culture**

Case study: Adapting to a new culture

Background Homebuild is an international furniture retail company, which operates in many countries in Europe, Asia-Pacific and the Americas. There is quite a lot of international mobility within the organisation, although managers are not always given a lot of preparation for their new roles.

Situation Inge Svensson has been appointed to the position of Regional Sales Manager in your country and has just relocated with her husband and two young children. She has not worked abroad before and is clearly not finding it easy to settle into her job or to establish herself as the head of the team. Although technically competent, her management style is very different from what the members of her new team are used to. For example, she wants everyone to spend a lot of time in meetings discussing departmental issues, until everyone agrees about what to do.
You have the opportunity to advise Inge. What can you tell her about:

- how managers are expected to behave in your country
- the key things to understand about life and work in your country which will help her establish herself more successfully?

Tasks 1 With a partner, draw up a list of key points which you wish to raise with Inge.
2 With another partner, role-play the meeting with her.
  You may like to use the list of possible areas below as a checklist. For example, you could talk about two or three of the areas under each heading which you think are important.

Structural	**Social**
geography	family
climate	gender roles
government	work–life balance
history	forms of address
religion	degrees of formality
attitudes to authority	taboos
regional differences	humour

At work	**Physical**
company organisation	physical space between people
the importance of hierarchy	physical contact
dress code	kiss, bow or shake hands?
punctuality	physical gestures
the working day	volume and speed of speech
meetings	
company communication	
decision-making and delegation	
the balance between the team and the individual	

3 Compare the points you identified with those of others in the group.

E Language reference

Glossary

allocate	distribute something for a special purpose, for example work tasks
blind spot	an area where a person's view is obstructed (for example, for a driver in a car); something that you don't know about yourself that other people know
hierarchy	a system of grades of authority from the lowest to the highest
kaizen	a Japanese business philosophy of continuous improvement of working practices
matrix organisation	one where employees report to more than one person
predictive	concerned with saying what will happen in the future
report (noun)	a team member who is responsible to a manager

Language summary

The Four Ps of business communication
Preparation
Purpose
Process
People

Stages in the communication process
1 Preparation
2 Opening
3 Relationship building
4 Structuring
5 Discussing and negotiating
6 Deciding
7 Concluding and summarising
8 Closing
9 Celebrating

Language for assessing yourself
I'm very / quite / rather / fairly / not very / not at all good at bringing people in during meetings.
I think I'm / I don't think I'm a good listener.
I'd say (that) I'm / I wouldn't say (that) I'm a good delegator.

Language learning tips

1 Planning
Create your own language improvement programme:
- How much time can you give it every day/week?
- What do you want to learn?
Look back at your diary regularly to see and measure the progress you are making.

2 Grammar
When you want to remember a grammar rule, always learn an example which is relevant to you as well as the rule.
Example: third conditional
If I hadn't missed the plane, I would have got to her party.
Remember, grammar is not an end in itself; it's a means towards an end.

Writing tasks

1 Review the management material in this unit, then write down six sentences which describe your strengths as a manager and six sentences which describe your weaknesses.

2 Look at the stages in the communication process above, then write an e-mail which is structured in line with the main steps 2–8.

F Tips for becoming a better manager

1 Take a few minutes to reflect on these two tips linked to the theme of this unit. How far do you agree with each one? Which do you think is most important, and which ideas are most useful?

TIP 1

Learning to be a good manager is a lifelong adventure. First, you need to decide whether you want to be a manager or not. There should be no stigma attached to the decision that management is not for you. But once you decide to set out on that journey, you have no idea how far you will travel, so it can be helpful and motivating to record your progress during your trip.

Ideas to help you on your lifelong management adventure:

● Measure your progress as a leader – keep a management diary and record your steps forward. Keeping a record of your route will show you where you have been and how far you have travelled.
● Set yourself regular challenges, both personal and professional.
● Review your progress from time to time. You will start to surprise and then to amaze yourself as you look back, and therefore look forward more positively.

TIP 2

Overcome your fears, and build your courage. Managing other people – especially when you are starting out – can make you feel stressed, anxious and insecure. Knowing yourself and developing belief in yourself will help you manage yourself and others.

Ideas to help you build your courage:

● Remember that good managers are not necessarily always nice, but they're fair. Trying to win friends among the people you manage is not the way.
● Try to set the tone from the start. Ask your people how they like to be managed. Tell them how you want to manage.
● Don't allow yourself to feel isolated. The challenges you face are probably similar to those of thousands of other managers. Find someone to support you – for example, get a mentor.

---

2 What other ideas for becoming a manager have you got from studying this unit?

Personal action plan 3 Think about what you have learned from this unit. Note down two or three important points which you want to apply to your own job (*What?*). Then create a schedule to implement your learning (*When?*) and think about the best way to check that you have successfully carried out your action (*How?*).

4 Discuss your personal action plan and adapt it if necessary, based on any useful feedback you get.

2 Building a team

People have become the main source of competitive advantage ... There are probably 100 studies out here showing that you get a 30 to 40 per cent productivity and profit advantage by treating people in the right way.

Jeffrey Pfeffer, Professor of Organizational Behavior, Stanford University

AIMS

A To develop team-building skills
B To improve social skills and build professional relationships
C To develop international leadership skills
D To examine cultural stereotyping and cultural differences

A Discussion and listening

Think about it

1 *Competitive advantage* means doing better than your competitors in business. Do you agree with Jeffrey Pfeffer (see the quote at the top of the page) that the best way to succeed is by treating your people well? What do you think he means by 'treating people in the right way'?

2 What can the leader of a new team do to show that (s)he means to treat people well?

Listen to this

3 🎧 **5** Anindita Gupta is an experienced business leader based in Mumbai, India. Listen to her talking about her ideas for building a successful team.

a What two aspects of building a team does she think are important?
b How does she get people to achieve the second of those aspects?
c What does she say are the four key aspects of people's approach to work which the Margerison-McCann Team Management Profile examines?
d What does Anindita say is another benefit of the Team Management Profile tool?

4 Now match each of the Types of Work in the diagram with one of the statements below.

1 Gathering and reporting information   *Advising*
2 Establishing and implementing
   ways of making things work
3 Controlling and auditing the
   working of systems
4 Creating and experimenting with ideas
5 Co-ordinating and integrating
   the work of others
6 Assessing and testing the
   applicability of new approaches
7 Upholding and safeguarding
   standards and processes
8 Exploring and presenting opportunities
9 Concluding and delivering outputs

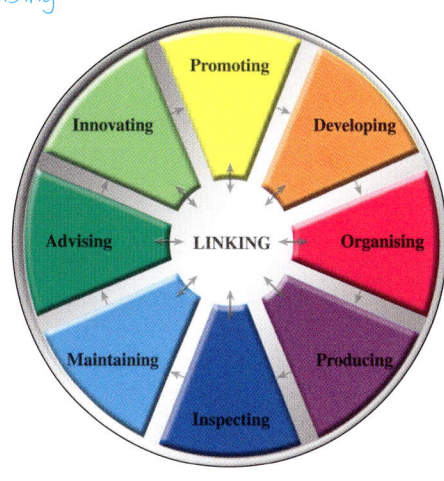

5 Discuss with a partner which areas of work you most enjoy.

Focus on language **6** Match the lists of words (1–5) with the phrases (a–e), according to how they form word combinations with *team*.

a team ....
b to .... a team
c a team of ....
d a team ....
e a(n) .... team

1 sales / management / creative / advisory / support / project
2 develop / lead / assemble / build / break up
3 effort / leader / player / member
4 experts / independent professionals / specialists / dedicated individuals
5 spirit / effort / participation / co-ordination

7 Complete these sentences with the correct form of the word *lead* from the box.

lead	leader	leadership	leading	led

a Johannes was a member of the research group, but is now the team ....
b Sarah will have to .... a team of ten people initially.
c Toni played a .... role in the takeover of the Spanish company last year.
d He is going to have to adapt his .... style if he wants his team to get
   better results.
e Joe .... the project for three years until his retirement.

8 Make sentences about yourself for each of the forms of *lead* and report them to the rest
of the group.

Let's talk **9** You have just joined a new organisation and have been given responsibility for a team of
ten people whom you do not know. With a partner, discuss your plan for getting to know
your team and for improving its effectiveness. Then present your plan together to the rest
of the group.

B Communication skills: Building relationships

Think about it **1** **Good working relationships are important for good results and are even more important in diverse international teams.**

    a How long have the people in your department been working together?

    b How well do they know each other?

    c Do colleagues often socialise together outside work?

Listen to this **2** 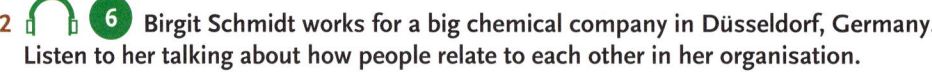 **Birgit Schmidt works for a big chemical company in Düsseldorf, Germany. Listen to her talking about how people relate to each other in her organisation.**

    a Birgit gives three examples of formality in professional relations in her company. What are they?

    b What does she say professional relations are based on?

    c How are things changing?

    d How does she feel about the changes?

3  **Now listen to how she sees people relating to each other in other parts of the organisation.**

    a What is a European Works Council (EWC)?

    b How do the members of this one communicate with each other?

    c How do professional relations differ in the EWC from the ones Brigit has at home?

    d What does Birgit think is the reason for the difference in professional relations between Germany and some other countries?

4 **Birgit talks about the more 'task-focused' style of some people and the more 'person-oriented' style of others. Which of these statements do you agree with more?**

    a I think it's important to keep work relations quite formal and to focus mainly on the tasks to be completed.

    b I think you need to really get to know people in order to work with them efficiently.

5 **Do you think you need to adapt your approach to tasks and people when you work internationally? What strategies do you use for building relationships internationally?**

Focus on language **6** **It is a critical skill to be able to tell people quickly and clearly who you are and what you do. Here is a checklist of strategies for the first stage of a professional introduction. Match the comments (a–e) with the headers in the box.**

Your name	Your job	Your organisation	Its activity	Your location

    a Have a sentence ready to explain this as clearly and briefly as possible.

    b The person you're talking to may not be familiar with people's names in your culture. Say it slowly and clearly, so that they can understand each syllable.

    c Think about how well the person is likely to know where you come from.

    d Think about whether the person you're talking to is likely to have heard of it or not.

    e You must know what it is in English. Make it clear whether it is preceded by *a* or *the*.

7 Look at these phrases for presenting yourself in a professional context. In each section, one of the phrases (a–c) is incorrect or inappropriate here. Decide which is the odd one out in each case.

1 **Your team**
   a There are five of us in the department.
   b I have a team of five people.
   c We are five persons.

2 **Your main responsibilities**
   a I'm responsible for the whole range of HR activities in the company.
   b I'm concerned by health and safety.
   c I'm in charge of finance.

3 **Your current projects**
   a Presently, I work on a big software project.
   b At the moment, I'm working on a new appraisal system.
   c Currently, I'm working on our internal communication.

4 **Your interests outside work**
   a In my free time, I like cooking and socialising with friends.
   b In my leisure, I like to see movies and read.
   c In my spare time, I like jogging and working out in the gym.

8 In their book *Communicating Internationally in English*, Bob Dignen and Ian McMaster identify a number of important strategies for socialising. First look at these examples (a–i) of socialising expressions used by someone at a conference. Then match them with one of the strategies (1–9) below.

a How about you?
b Really? That's very interesting.
c I'm an environmental engineer.
d You were in Miami? My brother works in Miami.
e Hello, are you on your own? Can I introduce myself?
f That's very funny. I must tell my colleagues that one.
g Have you been to an IPM conference before?
h GDF Suez? We work with them. Are you in environment, energy or gas?
i That must have been very challenging. How did you feel at the end of it?

1 Take the initiative.
2 Ask questions.
3 Show knowledge of the other person's working life.
4 Keep answers short.
5 Hand the conversation back by returning a question.
6 Listen actively.
7 Show empathy.
8 Respond positively to humour.
9 Find something in common.

9 Which of the strategies in Exercise 8 do you use? Which do you not use? When could you next use this list?

Let's talk **10** Either practise presenting yourself or give yourself a new identity, using the checklist on page 90. Choose a job and a country, etc. which are different from your own. Then role-play with a partner a first meeting during a coffee break at a leadership seminar which you are both attending in Tokyo. Get to know each other and start building a professional relationship.

C Professional skills: A model for team leadership

Think about it   **1**   **Some leaders regularly ask their team members these three questions.**

     a What am I doing that I shouldn't be doing?

     b What am I not doing that I should be doing?

     c What can I do to help you do your job better?

     Do you think they are good questions to ask? If you asked one of your team members these questions, what answers do you think you would get?

Read this   **2**   **Read the article below about the Developing People Internationally model, designed by York Associates. Then answer this question.**

     Which of the nine questions in the model deals with:

     a setting goals?   **c** defining roles?   **e** representing the team?

     b defining rules?   **d** coaching and mentoring?   **f** creating synergy?

The Developing People Internationally (DPI) model was developed by Jeremy Comfort of York Associates to help leaders and people working in international teams to be more aware of the key areas they need to pay attention to, in order to ensure that the team functions effectively. The DPI model consists of nine key questions and is a useful checklist for any work group to ask itself on a regular basis, from SMEs (small or medium-sized enterprises) to global multinationals.

1 Who are we?
The more that you and your team members know yourselves and each other, the better you will be able to play to the strengths of each team member. People who do what they like doing perform better. You will also be able to recognise gaps in the team more readily.

2 Where are we going?
All team members must be clear about their objectives. The more involved team members are in the definition of the team's objectives, the more committed they will be to realising them.

3 How do we plan to do it?
Teams need to know not only *what* they want to achieve but *how* they are going to achieve their goals. Planning, including agreement on how to work together and defining rules and procedures,

often proves to be the difference between successful and unsuccessful team working.

4 Who does what?
Defining roles is also critical. Knowing who likes doing what, and who is good at doing what (see question 1), is enormously helpful here.

5 What help is needed?
We know that leaders should support the members of their team. But when the team is project-based and/or virtual, possibly made up of people in a matrix organisation who do not answer directly to the team leader, then support in the form of coaching and mentoring may be neglected. Some individuals may then start feeling a sense of frustration and isolation.

6 How are we performing?
The key to assessing and raising performance is feedback. Good teams create a 'feedback culture'.

7 How are we seen in the organisation?
If the team does not have a visible profile in the wider organisation, it will not receive recognition, which is demotivating. It also may not get the resources needed to carry on doing a good job. Teams need ambassadors, who can represent them to the world outside the team.

8 Where are conflicts generated?
Conflict is not always destructive, but it often is. Team members need to build good relationships

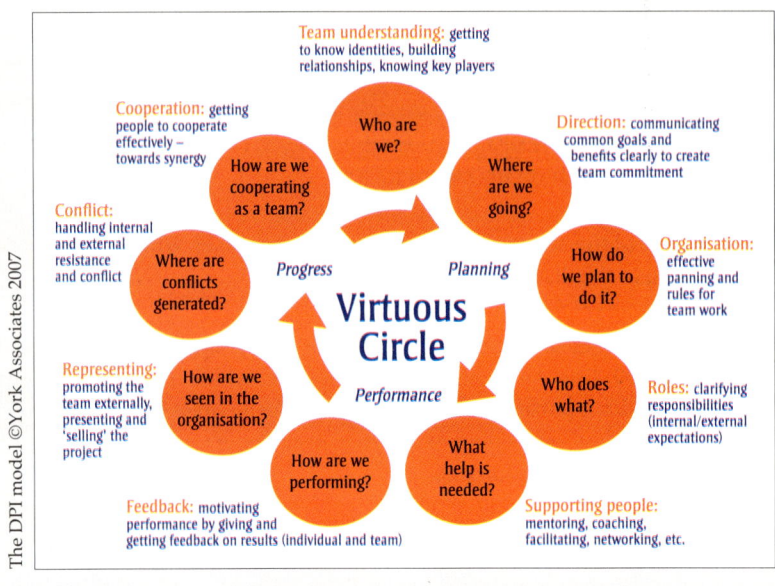

The DPI model ©York Associates 2007

so that when conflicts arise, the relationships are strong enough to withstand the strains that inevitably occur in any work situation. Helping people to understand how to deal with conflict is also beneficial to the team as a whole.

9 **How are we co-operating as a team?**
The aim of all this is for the team to improve its effectiveness and to get better results. The idea underpinning the whole model is that mutual understanding, support and good communication lead to greater synergy.

The tool is remarkably simple to use. You simply have to ask yourself how positive your answer to each question is; and you need to know how positive the answers of your team members are as well. It can be a powerful aid to team communication and for training and development. The more positive the answers, the more likely it is that your team is a high-performance one, delivering strong results. If there are any weak links in the chain, then you will be able to identify them collectively. And even if you feel that you are strong in most areas, there will always be room for improvement somewhere.

3 **Discuss these questions with a partner.**
   a How do you think you could use the DPI model in your organisation?
   b Where do you think you are strong and not so strong in terms of these different questions?
   c Can you give examples of best practice in any of these areas?

Focus on language 4 **Find words in the article to match these definitions.**
   a not communicating face to face (introduction)
   b lacks, intervals, differences separating two things (question 1)
   c caring a lot about something (question 2)
   d describing an organisation where employees can report to two different managers (question 5)
   e representatives of a team or country (question 7)
   f forming the basis for, supporting (question 9)
   g the combined effect of two or more things which is greater than their effects individually (question 9)
   h a simple description of a system (question 9)
   i connections (conclusion)

5 **These comments come from a team that is not working well. For each statement (a–i), identify the question in the article (1–9) which the team needs to address.**
   a 'I hardly know some of the people in the team .'
   b 'No one outside the team knows what we do.'
   c 'Some of us have a lot more work than others.'
   d 'I get an annual appraisal from my boss.'
   e 'No one really knows what we're supposed to be doing.'
   f 'People in our team usually feel low, unmotivated.'
   g 'Meetings are poorly organised, and when we do agree something, it's never followed up with action.'
   h 'There are always disputes about a number of things.'
   i 'I just don't think we work particularly well together. There's no synergy.'

Let's talk 6 **Look at the DPI model again. Discuss these questions with a partner, then report back to the group.**
   a How far can you give positive answers to each of the nine questions about the team you work in?
   b How do you think your colleagues in the team would answer these questions? Would they answer in the same way as you?
   c Which are the strong points in the way your team works?
   d Which are the weak points?
   e How could you make the work of your team more effective?

D Intercultural competence: Stereotypes and cultural differences

1 **Discuss how far you think these statements are true.**

   a The Chinese are very hard-working.

   b The British are bad at learning languages.

   c French waiters can be the rudest in the world.

   d Southern Europeans speak with their hands more than northern Europeans.

   Do you think stereotypes like these can serve a useful purpose, or do they lead us to unhelpful generalisations about groups of people?

2 **A graph like the one below helps us to avoid cultural stereotyping by modifying the kind of language we use to talk about different groups of people. Here we cannot say 'People from group X are always late for meetings'. We *can* say 'People from group X tend to arrive later for meetings than people from group Y.'**

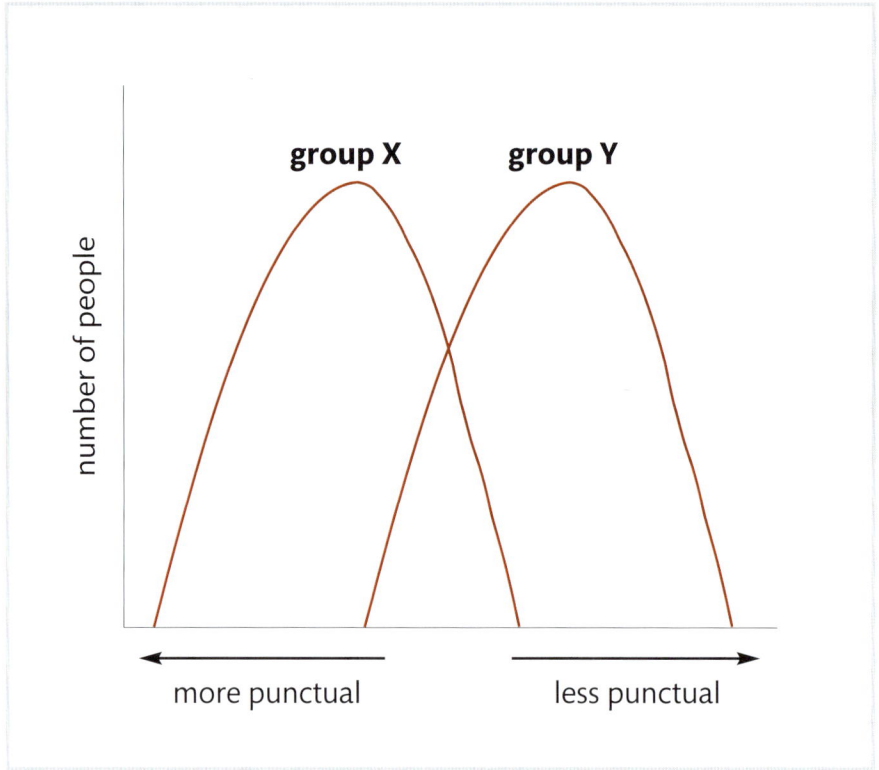

Keeping the graph in mind, write three statements which you think are true about three different groups of people – national, professional, etc. Test their acceptability on your partner.

3 **One important cultural and personal difference among people at work is between more task-oriented people and those who are more people-oriented. Read these definitions, then discuss the questions below with a partner and with the group.**

   ● Very task-oriented people want to get the job done and do not consider who they are working with to be so important.

   ● Those who are more people-oriented need to get to know the people they are working with before they can get on with the job.

   a How far do you feel that you are more task-oriented or more people-oriented at work?

   b How does this orientation vary, according to the situation?

Case study: Learning to work in a new culture

Background Naim Ahmad is Indian, in his mid-30s, with a background in marketing. He has a degree from a leading Indian business school and ten years' experience working in three different companies in Delhi. His latest move is to Switzerland, to work on brand development in the head office of a major international food company.

Situation Naim is enjoying the challenge of meeting demanding sales targets for the products he is working on and believes he can succeed. However, there are a number of aspects of his new job and working environment which he finds it difficult to adjust to:

- He does not feel that he has the opportunity to exchange ideas in meetings in the way he is used to. Some of his Swiss colleagues are getting impatient with the length of time that Naim wants to spend talking, when there is so much work to do.
- English is the working language for meetings. There are a number of other non-Swiss people in Naim's department. Sometimes he struggles to understand what they are saying and to make himself understood. This makes Zoe, a team member from New York, quite impatient.
- People leave the office much earlier here than Naim expected. He thinks that people here don't take their jobs as seriously as in India. His Swiss colleagues think that it's bad for the team as a whole if one person stays much later in the office than everyone else. They think that Naim is trying to impress the head of department by regularly working late.
- Naim is beginning to worry that a lack of commitment from other people may make it difficult for him to meet his targets. He is also beginning to wonder if he has made the right career decision by coming to Switzerland. His new colleagues are wondering the same.

Hello Sylvia,

Thanks for your e-mail. I'm fine, the weather's good and the snow is perfect for skiing! How's life in Rome?

I'll mention discreetly to Naim that you'd like a quicker response from him to your e-mails. He sometimes seems to have problems understanding us, so maybe he doesn't like writing in English.

In fact, we are a bit concerned about him. He only seems to think about work and doesn't join in any of our activities. I guess not being able to ski doesn't help! When he first arrived, he wanted to talk all the time in meetings, but we soon told him we had other things to do. Now he doesn't say much. It's true we haven't really figured out how to work with him yet. Anyway, I'll make sure he gets back to you.

All the best
Gerard

Task You have the opportunity to coach Naim in his new post.

1 Write down some of the questions that you would like him to consider.

2 What do you think may be some of the international competences that he is giving more and less focus to?

3 Discuss your views with a partner *or* role-play with a partner a coaching session between Naim and his coach.

Glossary appraisal   a judgment, evaluation or measurement of someone's job performance
stereotyping   putting forward a fixed idea or ideas about a person or group of people which is/are not completely true or accurate in reality

Language summary

Determining our preferences in the workplace
(from the Margerison-McCann Team Management Profile)

How you prefer to relate to others at work
Each day at work, you have to interact with others to get the work done. Some people like to do this in an **Extroverted** way, meeting frequently with others, talking through ideas, and enjoying a variety of tasks and activities. Other people, however, are more **Introverted**, preferring to think things through on their own before speaking, and generally not having a high need to be with others.

How you prefer to gather and use information
In the process of relating with others, people will gather and use various types of information. They do this either in a **Practical** or a **Creative** way. **Practical** information-gatherers prefer to work with tested ideas and pay attention to facts and details, whereas **Creative** information-gatherers are ideas-oriented and always looking for ways to change and improve things.

How you prefer to make decisions at work
Once the information is gathered, it is necessary to make decisions. Some people go about this in an **Analytical** way, setting objectives and choosing those decisions which best meet the objectives. Others may prefer to make decisions based on their **Beliefs**, where personal principles and values are more important.

How you prefer to organise yourself and others at work
Decisions have to be implemented within a team framework. Some people like a **Structured** environment, where things are neat and tidy and where action is taken quickly to resolve issues. Others prefer to be more **Flexible** and to make sure that all possible information has been gathered before decisions are taken. They prefer to find out about situations and delay taking action until they are sure that all alternatives have been explored.

Word combinations with *team*
- a sales team – a management team – a creative team – an advisory team – a support team – a project team
- to develop a team – to lead a team – to assemble a team – to build a team – to break up a team
- a team effort – a team leader – a team player – a team member
- a team of experts – a team of independent professionals – a team of specialists – a team of dedicated individuals
- team spirit – team effort – team participation – team coordination

Word combinations with *lead*
- a leading role – a leading authority – a leading businessperson
- lead a team – lead a project
- a great leader – a team leader – a deputy leader
- real leadership – leadership style – leadership training – leadership qualities

Language learning tips

Pronunciation
Having your own learner's English–English dictionary is useful for your pronunciation, as well as for vocabulary, especially since most of them come with a CD-ROM now.

1 Count the number of syllables of a word you are not sure about and consult the phonetic transcription in your dictionary to see which syllable gets the stress, e.g. *management* /ˈmænɪdʒmənt/: the ˈ comes before the stressed syllable.

2 Load the CD-ROM from your dictionary onto your PC so that you can call up a word and click on it to hear the correct pronunciation. Click and repeat what you hear several times. There are free online dictionaries where you can do this, too.

Writing task   Write a programme for a team-building day for your team.

F Tips for building a team

1 Take a few minutes to reflect on the two tips below linked to the theme of this unit. How far do you agree with each one? Which do you think is most important, and which ideas are most useful?

'The company's team-building retreat was where I was singled out and attacked!'

www.CartoonStock.com

TIP 1

Good leaders spend time thinking about how to improve their own performance, as well as thinking about how to improve the performance of their people.

Ideas to help you think about your own performance and the performance of others:

● Block out time to think. Put your thinking time in your planner so that you and others know that it is there.

● Find a regular place and time for thinking which suit you.

● If you have the luxury of space in your working environment, create different kinds of space for different kinds of interaction – where people can work on their own, where they can work with others formally, where they can meet informally, and where they can think. Change the geography of your workplace to suit the various needs that people have through the day.

TIP 2

Use the Developing People Internationally model regularly to check the health and productivity of your team. The nine key questions for team leaders and team members to address regularly are:

1 Who are we?
2 Where are we going?
3 How do we plan to do it?
4 Who does what?
5 What help is needed?
6 How are we performing?
7 How are we seen in the organisation?
8 Where are conflicts generated?
9 How are we co-operating as a team?

Ideas to help you integrate the DPI model into the life of your team:

● Ask yourself the nine questions on a regular basis.

● Try to know how other team members would answer these questions as well.

● If you are not sure, ask them to answer them more often as well!

---

2 What other ideas for building a team have you got from studying this unit?

Personal action plan 3 Think about what you have learned from this unit. Note down two or three important points which you want to apply to your own job (*What?*). Then create a schedule to implement your learning (*When?*) and think about the best way to check that you have successfully carried out your action (*How?*).

4 Discuss your personal action plan and adapt it if necessary, based on any useful feedback you get.

3 Getting and giving direction

A leader is best when people barely know he exists; not so good when people obey and acclaim him; worst when they despise him.

Lao Tzu, Chinese philosopher and founder of Taoism

AIMS

A To understand how to give direction

B To learn about communicating direction and communication styles

C To identify key skills for good leadership

D To examine the relationship between direction and hierarchy

---

A Discussion and listening

Think about it **1 Discuss these questions.**

a Do you agree with what Lao Tzu says about leadership?

b Are you clear about your own targets at work for the week? for the month? for the year? Are you clear about your department's or team's targets? Do you think everyone agrees what the team's targets are?

c How do organisations establish direction?

d Who sets the targets for individuals and teams in your organisation?

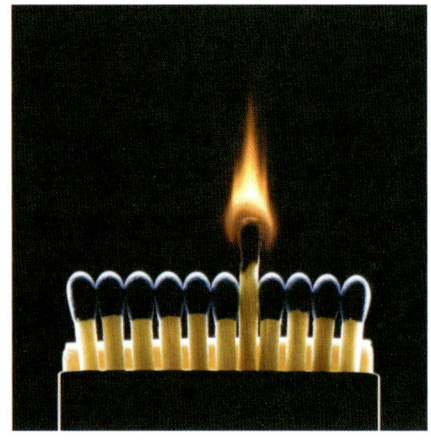

Listen to this **2** 🎧 **8** **Alfredo Diaz is a factory manager for the Mexican subsidiary of a German chemicals company based in Mexico City. Listen to him talking about how direction is established in his organisation and decide whether these statements are true or false.**

a Direction is weak in Alfredo's company.

b The company does not have statements of vision and values.

c Communication is as much bottom-up as top-down.

d There is a lot of reporting to head office.

e Alfredo has a directive management style.

f Production targets can be challenging.

3 🎧 **9** Eva Petersson is the administrator for an international construction project, managed by a Swedish engineering company in Stockholm. Listen to her talking about how direction is established in her organisation. Complete these sentences as you listen.

a Eva's job is to liaise between the management committee, the .... and the ....

b The main contractors are from Germany, ... and ....

c The goal of the project that Eva works on is to complete a major .... in the centre of Stockholm.

d The project leader .... the big decisions himself.

e Decision-making can take ....

f Communication is mainly .... - .... from the management committee to the zones.

4 Direction is established in different ways in the two organisations featured in Exercises 2 and 3.

a Which is your own organisation closer to?

b What are the main differences between your organisation and theirs?

c Does your organisation have a statement of its mission or values? If it does, what do you think of it? How useful is it? If it doesn't have one, should it?

Focus on language **5** Look at some of the terms Alfredo uses when talking about direction in his company. Complete the sentences below with words from the box.

| boardroom | cascading down | directive | intranet | process worker |
| shareholder value | shop floor | values | vision |

a A .... is someone who works on the production line of the factory.

b The .... of the company is a set of ideas about why it exists, what its people believe in, and where it wants to go.

c The .... of the company are a statement of what the organisation stands for, and what it believes is right and wrong.

d The company's .... is a private computer network which can usually only be accessed by the organisation's employees.

e A .... manager is one who mainly tells other people what to do.

f .... is the extra money investors in the company get from its successful performance.

g .... is a process by which information travels through an organisation

h The .... is the place where the directors of the company meet.

i The .... is the place in the factory where goods are made.

Let's talk **6** Henkel is a privately owned international company, headquartered in Düsseldorf, Germany, with 48,000 employees worldwide. These are its values.

> ▶ 1 We put our **customers** at the centre of what we do.
> ▶ 2 We value, challenge and reward our **people**.
> ▶ 3 We drive excellent, sustainable **financial** performance.
> ▶ 4 We are committed to leadership in **sustainability**.
> ▶ 5 We build our future on our **family** business foundation.

Think of a company you know well. Write a statement of its values and show it to your partner, without identifying the company. Can they guess which business it is? (If you need help with this, look up the mission statements of some well-known companies on the Internet.)

B Communication skills: Giving direction and communication styles

Think about it **1** In some organisations, information flows from the top down; in some, it flows from the bottom up; and in others, it flows in both directions. How is direction communicated in your organisation? Is it done well?

2 How do *you* communicate direction to colleagues?

Listen to this **3** 🎧 **10** Listen to Alfredo Diaz, the factory manager in Mexico from Section A, talking about how he communicates direction.
  a What are Alfredo's two rules for good communication?
  b What three questions does he ask himself when he talks to his staff?
  c How does Alfredo describe his own communication style?
  d What are Alfredo's two versions of K.I.S.S.?
  e What drives Alfredo crazy?

4 🎧 **11** Listen to Eva Petersson, the project administrator in Sweden from Section A, talking about how direction is communicated in her organisation.
  a How does Eva help the project leader?
  b What question does she ask herself when she is communicating with colleagues?
  c Does Eva prefer phoning, speaking face to face, or e-mailing as the best form of communication? Why?
  d Is Eva's communication mainly one way?
  e How does she describe her communication style?
  f How does she adapt her communication style to some of the contractors?

5 Eva says she learned to adapt her communication style when dealing with foreign contractors. How do you adapt your communication style to different people and situations?

6 To be successful, what should a good international communication style consist of?

Focus on language **7** Look at the communication styles in the box, then complete the pairs of sentences below with the appropriate communication style.

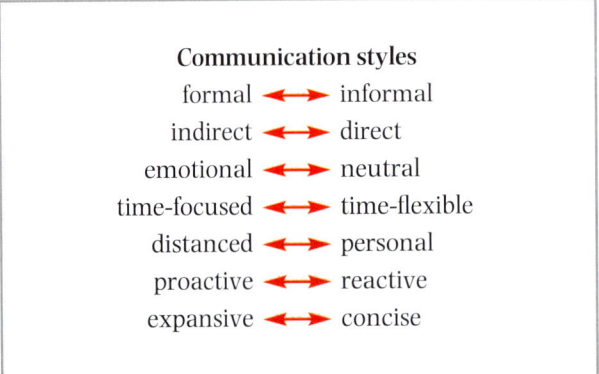

Communication styles
formal ⟷ informal
indirect ⟷ direct
emotional ⟷ neutral
time-focused ⟷ time-flexible
distanced ⟷ personal
proactive ⟷ reactive
expansive ⟷ concise

  a .... people use more traditional language, and have a conservative style.
     .... people have a more relaxed style, dress, body language, ...
  b .... people take the initiative.
     .... people wait for someone else to take the initiative.
  c .... people tend to use conditionals, modals, *possibly*, etc. to reduce impact.
     .... people use straight simple statements.
  d .... people show their feelings.
     .... people prefer not to show their feelings.

e .... people say more rather than less.

.... people say less rather than more.

f .... people think about the time while they talk.

.... people don't think about the time while they talk.

8 Below are some commentaries on ten 'golden rules' for good international communication, for both native and non-native speakers of English. Complete them with the golden rules from the box.

Avoid idiom.	~~Keep It Short and Simple.~~
Avoid local cultural references.	Speak slowly.
Be direct.	Summarise.
Check and clarify frequently.	Take turns when you speak.
Don't try to be funny.	Use simple words.

1 _Keep It Short and Simple_ (K.I.S.S.)

The first rule of business communication in English. Use simple structures and short sentences.

2 ....

If you speak English well and have a wide vocabulary, you could be using words that some other people in the meeting don't know. Look out for incomprehension.

3 ....

Avoid complicated expressions which may be difficult to understand or interpret.

4 ....

Take your time. Clear and careful pronunciation can make it much easier for people who have difficulty understanding the language of the meeting.

5 ....

Humour can often result in confusion, misunderstanding and lengthy explanations of jokes.

6 ....

Both national and organisational ones. Remember that outsiders do not share the knowledge and experience which you share with people from the same country, organisation or profession.

7 ....

Native speakers who use, for example, military or sporting metaphors, like *coming from left field* (from baseball), often do not realise that these are incomprehensible to most non-native speakers.

8 ....

It is both a courtesy and a good strategy for effective communication to ensure that everyone is following what is being said.

9 ....

A good meeting chair may decide to do this at the end of every point on the agenda.

10 ....

It's very difficult to follow a discussion in a foreign language when several people are talking at the same time.

Let's talk **9** Work with a partner. Look at the more detailed communication styles profile on page 92. Tell your partner which of each pair of words you think best describes his or her communication style. Then reverse roles. Discuss situations where you disagree.

C Professional skills: What makes a great boss?

Think about it **1** What do you look for in a manager? What do you think is a common strength and a common weakness among managers in your country or organisation?

2 Do you know a manager whom you would enter for a Best Boss competition in your country?

Read this **3** Read the article below about what people in the UK want from their bosses and then complete the table with information from the article.

'Some men are born great, some achieve greatness, and some are allowed to work for great men like me'

www.CartoonStock.com

	quality in order of importance To be:	% importance	% of managers seen as competent
1			
2			28
3	supportive		
4			
5		76	

British Best Boss awards

Do employees want firm leadership or sensitive people skills from their managers? First direct's research into Britain's workplaces reveals that people want the best of both worlds.

What do you want from your boss? The chances are it's a little bit more than just a pat on the back and a box of chocolates at the end of the year. But do you want the same things as the people around you? Or, for that matter, as the rest of the UK workforce?

The ideal boss

First direct's recent survey asked British employees from a range of sectors what they thought were the most valuable qualities in a manager – and it turns out most of us are seeking the same thing.

Topping the list was approachability, with 83% of those surveyed saying this was important. As anyone who has worked for an unapproachable boss can confirm, this is a key quality for a manager and something which really can make a difference to your working life.

Second most important, with 82% of respondents choosing it, was the skill of good communication. In our increasingly screen-led world, communication is more vital than ever and yet something many bosses struggle with. Talking often takes second place, as bosses are much more likely to fire off an e-mail instead.

Although 81% of those questioned also said they wanted their boss to be supportive, being a good leader also ranked highly, with 80% of those surveyed saying it was important. These findings clearly signal that employees want a caring and sharing boss, as well as someone who can give the orders and get the team moving in the right direction.

Finally, 76% of employees surveyed said that they wanted a boss who respects the individuality of their staff members.

The reality

Unfortunately, such perfect bosses are difficult to find in the real world. Although approachability was seen as a crucial quality, only 50% of respondents said their boss was approachable; while just 28% described their boss as a good communicator. Perhaps even more worryingly, only 38% of respondents said their boss was supportive, suggesting that there are a lot of uncaring, unsympathetic bosses out there. Additionally, just 31% of bosses were perceived as good leaders and only 36% were seen as respecting their staff as individuals.

Overall, it seems that there are many average bosses around who could certainly improve on their approachability, communication and leadership skills, while trying harder to treat their staff as individuals.

adapted from www. guardian.co.uk

4 How do you think you rate on each of the five qualities identified in the survey? How do you think other people would rate you?

5 Are these the qualities that you think are most important in a boss, or are other qualities more important?

Focus on language 6 Find words or phrases in the article which mean the same as these. (The words and phrases you are looking for occur in the same order in the article.)

a someone who is difficult to talk to

b computer-dominated

c find difficult

d quickly write and send

7 Decide whether the words below are used to talk about leaders or followers (the people they lead in organisations).

leaders	followers
superior	report

superior   report   worker   boss   director

executive   co-worker   employer   employee

team leader   wage earner   supervisor   subordinate

head   foreman   manager   staff member

8 Do you prefer to describe yourself as a leader or as a follower?

Let's talk 9 You are a management consultant. Your client company wants you to improve management skills, based on employees' assessments of those skills. Use the table on page 91 to decide on a management development programme for the company which you are consulting for.
Discuss with your partner what you will do over a 12-month period, draw up an action plan, and present it together to the rest of the group.

D Intercultural competence: Direction and hierarchy

1 Do this activity with a partner.

1 Share a single pen or pencil and, with both of you holding the pen at the same time, draw a house on a blank sheet of paper. You're encouraged to talk!

2 After two or three minutes, turn the paper over and, without talking, draw a house together from a different part of the world.

3 Teams should now present and talk about their houses.

Then discuss these questions.

a How did you draw your house?

b What were the barriers to doing the task?

c Did talking help or not?

d In what ways were you aware of the relationship with your partner? How did it feel to lead/follow?

e Did this remind you of any other situations you find yourself in?

f How can you use what you have learned here?

Thanks to Jim Chamberlain for telling the author about this activity.

2 Read this description of Hofstede's theory of 'power distance'. Then read the statements below (a–j) and decide whether each one is more characteristic of a member of a low or of a high power-distance culture.

In the 1970s, Geert Hofstede developed ideas about cultural difference based on his surveys of thousands of IBM managers. One of the dimensions he identified as important in understanding cultural difference he called 'power distance', which he defined as 'the extent to which the less powerful members of institutions and organisations within a country expect and accept that power is distributed unequally.'

Hofstede argued that in low power-distance cultures, people expect and accept power relations that are more consultative or democratic. They relate to one another more as equals, regardless of formal positions. In high power-distance countries, the less powerful accept power relations that are more autocratic and paternalistic. Subordinates acknowledge the power of others simply based on where they appear in formal, hierarchical positions. So his power-distance index reflects the way people perceive power differences.

a Senior managers shouldn't be getting so much more money than the average salary here. It's just not fair.

b The company is strong because control is centralised by head office.

c Orders come from above.

d The boss always arrives last at the meeting and always takes the chair.

e Local subsidiaries have a lot of autonomy.

f It's right that the CEO is paid a lot more than us. He has a lot more responsibility than we do.

g She shares an office with us.

h It's difficult to tell who the boss is in the meeting. He dresses and behaves just like everyone else.

i She consults us on every big decision.

j He has a big office on the top floor.

3 Do you think a) your organisation and b) your country tend to be examples of lower or higher power-distance cultures? Do you think that power distance is increasing or decreasing in each case?

4 What influence does power distance have in your organisation on how direction is decided and communicated?

Case study: Establishing direction

Before you read the case study, read this e-mail from a manager to his new departmental team.

> Hello everyone,
> I'd like to create an opportunity for me to get to know you all better, so I would like to organise an away-day one Saturday quite soon – certainly within the next month. My idea is to go to a hotel with nice facilities not too far from Paris and spend the day doing some team-building activities, discussion and informal socialising over a nice lunch and dinner. If anyone wants to stay over on Saturday night, I'll be more than happy to join them and continue into Sunday – there'll be tennis, swimming and golf, etc. to enjoy – although I appreciate that many of you have family and other commitments, so that a whole weekend may not be possible for all of you.
> Looking forward to hearing from you – and seeing you soon in quite different surroundings!
> Best wishes,
> Toni

Background Toni is an enthusiastic young Italian sales and marketing manager. He has recently got a job with an international construction company to manage a project in a new region with big potential. He has some experience of leading a team in Milan, but this is his first experience of working abroad and in this sector. His team consists of five people, four of whom are older than him. Two are French, one is American, one is Argentinian and one is Moroccan. The last two have worked for the company in Paris for several years. The people in the team get on well together. However, senior managers think that the team is rather settled in its ways and could be more productive.

Situation Toni plans to improve the team's motivation and has decided to hold a team-building activity. His aim is to get to know his people and for them to get to know each other better. He also wants to identify a clear direction for the project. He has taken part in similar events in Italy, and they worked well.

However, none of the other team members is convinced of the value of an away-day and all are busy with other work. They say they:

- have families and little spare time at the weekend
- are not paid to work at weekends
- think that team building is just a fashion.

Toni is upset by the lack of response to his e-mail, but when he repeats his request, one of the team complains to Toni's boss.

Task Discuss the case in small groups from the point of view of Toni's boss and decide what you would say in a meeting with Toni. Then compare your suggestions with those of the other groups.
You could also role-play this meeting or a meeting between Toni and his team. Appoint an observer to provide feedback after the meeting.

E Language reference

Glossary

boardroom	the place where the company's directors, who represent the shareholders, meet
cascading down	a form of communication in which the top layer of an organisation communicates a message to the next layer which then does the same and so on down so that the information flows down the organisation from top to bottom
directive	an official order or instruction, e.g. the European Union Working Hours Directive
intranet	an internet-based network for the communication of information within an organisation
mentee	someone who is mentored
mentor	someone who supports a younger, less experienced professional in his or her longer-term professional development
process worker	someone who works on the factory shop floor
shop floor	the part of the factory where manufacturing takes place

Language summary

Forms of *direct*

direct	directly	directorate
direction	directness	directorship
directive	director	directory

Word combinations with *direct*

direct action	direct tax	direct marketing
direct debit	direct cost	
direct method	direct line	

Language learning tips

Reading

Reading is a fantastic way of improving your vocabulary and your English in general. Use these tips to help you.

- Read actively with a highlighter.
- Don't just highlight individual words, highlight groups of words. Look at how words combine.
- Practise reading aloud for a few minutes every day. It's good for your pronunciation and for your fluency.
- Read lots of simple English. Read readers (books written for non-native speakers of English at different levels). Read at a level where you forget you are reading in English.
- Listen to the audio version at the same time as you read a reader.
- Read the English language version of your company's website.
- Subscribe to a free online newsletter in the area in which you work.

When could you read more English?

Writing task

Your mentee has asked you to advise him/her on how to get better direction in the team that he/she has recently started to lead. Write an e-mail with guidelines for good practice in establishing and maintaining clear direction.

F Tips for getting and giving direction

1 Take a few minutes to reflect on the two tips below linked to the theme of this unit. How far do you agree with each one? Which do you think is most important, and which ideas are most useful?

www.CartoonStock.com

TIP 1

Whether you work internationally or not, be aware of personal and cultural differences within the team:
- How far do people expect direction to come from above? How far do people want a say in the definition of the team's direction?
- How far do people want a plan? How far are people happy to live with less formal structure?
- How far do people want a push or a pull style of leadership?

Ideas to help you establish direction in a diverse context:
- Think about the questions above and formulate a leadership approach based on your answers to them.
- Spend time reflecting on the direction you want for yourself and your team. Make notes. Consult on your ideas. Formulate an action plan. Then communicate the final version effectively to all team members.

TIP 2

You and your team need to have a direction – you all need to know where you are going, and the team leader must be able to communicate that sense of direction.
The basis of good communication is clear communication.
Ten golden rules for good international communication are:

1 Keep It Short and Simple (K.I.S.S.).   6 Avoid local cultural references.
2 Use simple words.   7 Avoid idiom.
3 Be direct.   8 Check and clarify frequently.
4 Speak slowly.   9 Summarise.
5 Don't try to be funny.   10 Take turns when you speak.

---

2 **What other ideas for getting and giving direction have you got from studying this unit?**

Personal action plan 3 **Think about what you have learned from this unit. Note down two or three important points which you want to apply to your own job (*What?*). Then create a schedule to implement your learning (*When?*) and think about the best way to check that you have successfully carried out your action (*How?*).**

4 **Discuss your personal action plan and adapt it if necessary, based on any useful feedback you get.**

4 Organising teams

When dealing with people, remember you are not dealing with creatures of logic, but creatures of emotion.

Dale Carnegie, author of *How to Win Friends and Influence People*

AIMS

A To develop your ability to organise people
B To make meetings more efficient and effective
C To increase the engagement of your people
D To provide insights into the culture of organisations

A Discussion and listening

Think about it

1 How much of your time do you spend planning and organising your own work and the work of others?

2 Are you good at delegation (passing work on to others to do)?

3 What do you think are the main challenges for a manager when it comes to organising and planning?

Listen to this

4 🎧 **12** Fernando Ortiz is the leader of a group of engineers working for a Mexican mobile telecoms company in Guadalajara. Listen to him talking about how he organises his team, then answer these questions.

   a Why does Fernando say that organising is so important?
   b How does he define management?
   c How much time does he spend on planning?
   d How much time does he spend on communicating the plans?
   e What does he say is the difference between delegation and empowerment?
   f What is his biggest challenge as an organiser?

5 Discuss with your colleagues how Fernando's organisation of his team compares with your work situation. Consider the different topics he covers:

- Planning
- Delegation
- Empowerment
- Defining rules and procedures (for example, for meetings)
- Communication
- Debriefing and planning meetings

6 Complete these sentences using the correct form of the word *organise*.

a Petra is a fantastic .... She looks after all our big meetings, seminars and sales conferences.

b Natasha, on the other hand, is not very well .... You only have to look at the state of her desk to see that!

c We'd like to give you more time for this project, but unfortunately there are .... constraints which stop us from doing so.

d Can we .... a meeting for sometime next week?

e This is very interesting, but we have to meet the needs of the .... first.

7 Use one of the forms of *organise* from Exercise 6 with each of these groups of words.

a .... a farewell dinner, ... a party

b an .... group of workers, poorly ....

c .... needs, ... requirements

d a business .... , an umbrella ....

e a union .... , a good ....

8 a In his article *Seven Failings of Really Useless Leaders*, Steven Sonsino identifies the things that incompetent managers damage through their action or behaviour. In this box are the seven things that are damaged. Use them to complete the table below. You can check some of the difficult words in the Glossary on page 46.

| culture | emotion | enthusiasm | engagement |
| explanation | reward | trust | |

what useless leaders damage	how they do it
a	micro-management; coercion; disrespect
b	aggression; lack of sensitivity and empathy; poor work–life balance
c	partial, inconsistent communication
d	individual objectives dictated by managers; limited team goals
e	rewarding the wrong things and offering the wrong sort of reward (e.g. money for someone not motivated by money)
f	ignoring the difference in cultures during mergers and acquisitions; punishing risk-taking while trying to introduce a culture of innovation
g	unfair recruitment or reward decisions

b Compare your answers with a partner. If you chose different words for any of the categories, explain your choices. Then check in the key on page 107.

9 In the same article, Steven Sonsino proposes how other managers can avoid the traps that really incompetent managers fall into. In pairs or small groups, discuss what managers can do to encourage these things in their teams.

- positive emotion
- enthusiasm
- a strong culture
- explanation and clear communication
- fair rewards
- engagement
- respect and trust

Then report back to the whole group. (You can also compare your ideas with Steven Sonsino's in the answer key on page 107.)

B Communication skills: Organising meetings

Think about it **1** Discuss these questions with a partner.

    a How much time do you spend in meetings every week?

    b How much time do you waste in meetings every week? Why?

Listen to this **2** 🎧 **13** Oleg Varushkin and Renate Bierhoff work in the Kiev office of a European packaging company. They both report to an English manager, Nick Smith. They are unhappy about the lack of preparation for their monthly departmental meeting. Listen to their conversation.

    a What do they think is the main problem?

    b Which of these factors do they also mention?

        1 Purpose of meeting unclear ☐

        2 Identity of those attending unclear ☐

        3 Roles unclear ☐

        4 Documentation not distributed in advance ☐

        5 Room not booked ☐

        6 Items on agenda are ambiguous ☐

        7 Nick's punctuality ☐

        8 Agenda not stating a finishing time for meeting ☐

        9 Refreshments not provided ☐

3 How are meetings prepared for in your organisation? Do you think enough time is spent on preparation?

Focus on language **4** Match each header in the box with the written information below about a meeting that Nick has organised.

> documentation   facilities   people and roles   place
> purpose and content   time   type of meeting

a ....
The next meeting of the AYB/5 project group will take place in room B505 on May 5.
To find Block B, access the map on the intranet.

b ....
The meeting will start at 14.00 and finish at 17.00 with a 15-minute break at 15.30.

c ....
All members of the project group are expected to attend.
The meeting will be chaired by Nick Smith.

d ....

The objectives of the meeting are to finalise budget for Phase 3 of the project and identify cost overruns for Phase 2.

e ....

The meeting will be mostly a discussion of the budget, but there will be also be a briefing from Nick on Phase 2 costs, and we will spend some time brainstorming how to avoid further cost overruns in Phase 3.

f ....

A computer and projector will be available for presenters.
Tea and coffee will be provided before the meeting and during the break.
Cars may only be parked in the Block B car park if you obtain permission from corporate security at least one week before.

g ....

The agenda and all other relevant documents will be distributed one week beforehand. Participants should all have access to Phase 2 final budget and Phase 3 draft budget during the meeting.

5 Some meetings have different stages and purposes. For example, the first part may involve brainstorming, the second part may require a decision, etc. Match these different types of meeting (a–j) with their descriptions (1–10).

a a chance meeting
b a chat
c a brainstorming session
d a briefing
e an information exchange
f a decision-making meeting
g a discussion
h a planning meeting
i a problem-solving meeting
j a project meeting

A meeting ...

1 to tell people what they need to know
2 to tell people what they need to know and for them to respond
3 which takes place spontaneously
4 by the coffee machine
5 to throw up as many ideas as possible in a short time
6 to define an action plan
7 to resolve an issue
8 to get an update on work done and to check the schedule
9 to talk things through
10 to define the next stages in the process

6 Which types of meeting do you take part in most often? Are people always clear about the objectives of the meetings you organise?

Let's talk **7** You are going to suggest and discuss some ideas for reducing the amount of time spent in meetings. Divide into two groups, A and B, and look at the relevant page. When you have discussed the topic in smaller groups, come together for a discussion as a whole group.

Group A: Turn to page 91.
Group B: Turn to page 95.

C Professional skills: Female leadership and building engagement

Think about it **1 Discuss these questions.**

    a What is the image of the ideal leader in your organisation? What are the main qualities that leaders are expected to show?

    b What is the ratio of female to male leaders in your organisation? Do you think there are enough women leaders?

    c Do you think that a quota system is the best way to get more women into leadership positions?

    d Do you think that women typically show different leadership qualities than men? If so, what are they?

Read this **2 Beverly Alimo-Metcalfe is the professor of leadership at the University of Bradford School of Management in the UK. She has done a lot of research into the ways in which male and female leaders are seen, and differences between male and female leadership style. As you read her article on page 43, think about your answers to these questions:**

What is/are, according to the author:

    a the reason why women do not reach senior positions in organisations?

    b the problem with most leadership research up to now?

    c the heroic model of leadership?

    d female leadership typically based on?

    e 'servant leadership'?

    f the advantages of servant leadership for an organisation?

Professor Beverly Alimo-Metcalfe

3 Do you agree or disagree with the author's findings? Would you like to see a stronger culture of engaging leadership in your organisation or in your country?

Focus on language **4 Find words or phrases in the article that mean the same as the following.**

    a controversial, likely to cause disagreement (paragraph 1)

    b treat someone in a way that shows you feel superior to them (paragraph 1)

    c easily influenced by (paragraph 2)

    d someone who saves us from danger or failure (paragraph 4)

    e anyone who has a direct interest in the success of a particular business (paragraph 7)

    f integrate, fix deeply and firmly (paragraph 7)

    g measured, assessed (paragraph 8)

    h explained by, seen to be caused by (paragraph 9)

5 Match each of these words from the article (a–f) with a definition (1–6).

    a a quota

    b a level playing field

    c gender bias

    d a seismic change

    e a tsunami

    f proactivity

    1 a huge wave caused by an undersea earthquake

    2 making things happen rather than waiting for things to happen

    3 a fair situation, one where everyone can compete according to the same rules

    4 a limited number of people which is officially allowed

    5 a situation where members of one sex get better treatment than the other

    6 a massive shift

Why staff rate female leaders highly, but male bosses score them lower than men

A leadership study undertaken by Real World Group, and presented at Oxford Brookes University Women and Leadership Conference, shows gender issues still dominate perceptions of what makes a good boss.

by Professor Beverly Alimo-Metcalfe, Professor of Leadership, University of Bradford School of Management; Emeritus Professor of Leadership Studies, University of Leeds; CEO, Real World Group

The topic of quotas is one of the most contentious issues relating to ways of increasing the representation of women in senior positions in organisations. Those who disagree with quotas typically state that they patronise women and that they would far rather achieve promotion on a 'level playing field'. What they ignore, however, is that the playing field is far from level.

Why? Because the path through an organisation to the highest levels is marked by assessment processes – selection, promotion, appraisal – which are highly susceptible to gender bias.

When selecting individuals for the top, organisations are influenced by current thinking about the nature of leadership. The history of leadership research, dominated by US work, has been based on studies of men, by men. The absence of women has been virtually ignored by academics.

For the last few decades, in which chief executives of large US companies became the focus of study, heroic models of leadership have dominated leadership thinking; that is, notions of larger-than-life, charismatic individuals who excite others to follow them. 'Followers' are relegated to the role of passive recipients of these charms, who rely on the leader as 'the saviour'!

In general, research has found that women are more likely to adopt an approach to leadership which is based on genuine empowerment – as a partnership, in which the views of the staff are taken seriously.

Notions of leadership are affected by social, political, economic and technological change, and heroic models are now under attack, not least because corporate and political scandals have largely destroyed trust in the integrity of many of those in power. There has been a seismic change in our understanding of leadership, replacing notions of heroic with the idea that leadership resides in the relationships between, and co-operation among, individuals, regardless of role or level in an organisation. The global 'financial tsunami' resulting in the need to 'get more for less' means that mere 'followership' will not enable organisations to maximise the potential leadership needs of their staff; we now need to focus on 'employee engagement' and encouraging 'proactivity' in all.

Our major three-year investigation of leadership sought the views of staff rather than asking senior managers why they are effective. It has resulted in what we believe is the first model of 'engaging leadership', and closely resembles 'servant leadership'; that is, the notion that leaders create an environment and relationships which are based on genuine respect, empowerment, collaboration and partnership with their staff, colleagues and other stakeholders, in achieving the organisation's goals. In a subsequent three-year research study, we found that teams that embed a culture of engaging leadership are more productive, have higher morale and lower stress levels than those that don't.

While this should lead to optimism in relation to the increased opportunities for women to display their generally preferred style of leadership, I am still holding my breath. Why? Because additional research, conducted by Juliette Alban-Metcalfe of Real World Group, that compared how female and male middle-to-senior managers were rated by their bosses found that women were rated significantly lower than men. Interestingly, and importantly, their staff and colleagues rated them higher!

What might be the reason for these findings? Research studies revealed that even when women produced superior outcomes at work, this was more likely to be attributed to luck, or exerting extra effort, whereas men's success was more likely to be attributed to their personal capability. However, failure in women is more likely to be attributed to lack of ability, but for men, to bad luck.

A major problem for women is that they often challenge the preconceptions of the existing 'gatekeepers' in organisations (predominantly male senior managers) simply because they don't look like the notion of a leader, because to them, leaders look like them, i.e. men.

Let's talk 6 The senior management of the organisation where you work (or of an organisation that you know) has decided that it wants to increase the number of women in middle and senior leadership positions. They have appointed you and your colleagues to make recommendations as to how to achieve this. In groups, draw up an action plan with targets and a time scale to present to the senior management committee of the company.

D Intercultural competence: Organisational culture

1 Discuss these questions.

  a How is your organisation seen by other people?

  b Does the image that other people have of it match the image that those inside the organisation have of it?

  c What does an organisation need to make it a great place to work?

2 Before you look at the checklist below, brainstorm with a partner or small group what you think are the main ways in which the culture of an organisation can be described.

3 Describe the main characteristics of the culture of your organisation or your part of the organisation to a colleague. Use the relevant factors in this checklist to help you.

> ### Some characteristics of organisational culture
>
> - Nationality
> - Sector
> - Size (annual turnover, number of employees)
> - Location of headquarters
> - Ownership
> - Company structure
> - Dominant functions
> - Predominant management/leadership styles
> - Main communication processes and channels
> - Power distance
> - Main stakeholders
> - General working atmosphere
> - Dress style
> - Employee relations
> - Career development policy
> - Brand image
> - Mission and values

4 Are there any aspects of your organisation's culture which you would like to change? Imagine that you and your colleague(s) have been commissioned to work on changing the culture of your organisation. Identify the features of the culture which you wish to focus on and draw up a programme to bring about the changes you want to see.

5 What impact can _you_ have on the culture of your organisation?

Case study: Interpolis

1 **Read about some aspects of the culture of Interpolis, then answer the questions below.**

Interpolis is one of the largest insurance companies in the Netherlands. The company has gained wide recognition with its advertising campaign 'Interpolis. Crystal clear'.

In addition to insurance, Interpolis is also known for its special attitude to work. No one at Interpolis has their own fixed work space. The employees can select a place of work that is best suited to them and to the job that they do.

Special areas called 'club houses' have also been created at the Interpolis head office, each with its own particular atmosphere. In these club houses, the Interpolis employees can combine various daily activities, such as working, consulting, meeting people, relaxing and eating.

This flexible working concept led to a cultural transition at Interpolis. That is because flexible working is not just a matter of moving some furniture around. Flexible working must also become embedded in the way employees think and act.

Employees at Interpolis do not have to clock in for work. The motto at Interpolis is 'As long as the work gets done'. Whether it is done from home or at the office is something employees can decide for themselves. Interpolis is a pioneer of teleworking in the Netherlands. At present, about 2,500 employees work from home several days a week.

a People at Interpolis 'hot-desk'. What in the article tells us this?
b What type of flexible working is there at Interpolis?
c Why do Interpolis people have more than one place to work in the office?
d What is the Interpolis motto?
e What is 'teleworking'?

2 **Work space is an important aspect of the culture of any organisation. How similar is Interpolis to your workplace?**

3 **Does your organisation operate a system of flexible working? If not, should it?**

4 **Describe the typical work spaces of people in your organisation. How well adapted are they to your professional and personal needs? Imagine that your organisation is relocating to brand new premises and that you have been invited to discuss with the architects the working environment which will work best for you. What does your ideal work space look like?**

E Language reference

Glossary

acquisition	a company or part of a company bought by another; the process of one company buying another
coercion	the action of making someone do something by force or threats
emotional intelligence	the ability to understand and control one's own emotions and understand those of others
empathy	the ability to imagine and share another person's feelings
merger	when two companies or organisations join to form a larger one
micro-management	management with too much control or attention to detail
partial	not complete; showing too much favour to one person or group

Language summary

The 'useless leader' checklist

demanding	never gives praise
secretive	doesn't consult
doesn't delegate	interferes in work of reports
direct	takes credit for work of reports
critical of people's work	a poor listener
resists change	doesn't take decisions

Forms of *organise*

organise	organised
organiser	organisational
organisation	

Types of meeting
ad-hoc meeting
AGM (Annual General Meeting (BrE) / annual meeting (AmE))
board meeting (BrE)
brainstorming meeting
briefing meeting
chat
decision-making meeting
departmental meeting
discussion meeting
EGM (Extraordinary General Meeting)
executive committee meeting
information (exchange) meeting
off-site meeting
one-to-one meeting
planning meeting
problem-solving meeting
project meeting
staff meeting
stand-up meeting
works council meeting

Language learning tips

Using DVDs to improve your listening comprehension
Watch English-language films on DVD. It may be helpful to watch films that you already know in your own language. Watch your film in English:
1 with sub-titles in your own language;
2 with English sub-titles;
3 without sub-titles.

It works!

Writing task

Organising the team
Your manager has asked you to draw up a set of rules for the organisation of your team's work. Write down:
1 four things you think are good about the organisation of your team's work;
2 four things you think are not so good about the organisation of your team's work;
3 rules to deal with the biggest weaknesses.

Compare and discuss what you have written with others in the group.

RAM CHARAN

Co-author of the bestselling *Execution*

KNOW -HOW

The 8 Skills That Separate People Who Perform from Those Who Don't

1 Take a few minutes to reflect on the eight skills for leaders which Ram Charan identifies in his book *Know-How: The 8 Skills That Separate People Who Perform from Those Who Don't*. How far do you agree with each tip? Which do you think is most important, and which are most useful?

1 Know how to position the business to make money.

2 Connect what is happening in the outside world to what is happening in your business.

3 Manage the 'social system' of your business effectively so that people can work together more effectively.

4 Judge, select and develop future leaders of your business.

5 Mould a team of leaders: create 'unity without uniformity'.

6 Choose and set the right goals.

7 Set clearly marked-out priorities which will help achieve these goals.

8 React positively when forces beyond your control make themselves felt.

Very few of us master all of these in a lifetime but they are good targets to aim at!

2 What other ideas for organising a team have you got from studying this unit?

Personal action plan 3 Think about what you have learned from this unit. Note down two or three important points which you want to apply to your own job (*What?*). Then create a schedule to implement your learning (*When?*) and think about the best way to check that you have successfully carried out your action (*How?*).

4 Discuss your personal action plan and adapt it if necessary, based on any useful feedback you get.

5

Defining roles

We all know what distinguishes a good employer from a bad one. A good one provides four basic things. First, it makes sure that everyone has a proper job to do. Second, it pays them fairly. Third, it makes employees feel that their efforts are recognised. And fourth, it gives them nice people to work with.

Lucy Kellaway, British journalist

AIMS

A To clearly define roles for people
B To improve international negotiating skills
C To be able to influence people
D To consider the skills needed to work internationally

A Discussion and listening

Think about it **1** **How would you describe your main roles in your:**
a organisation?
b department?

How do you think your colleagues would describe them?

Listen to this **2** 🎧 **14** **Indira Kapoor is the International Marketing Manager for an Indian food company, which is expanding internationally. She is based in Delhi and is a member of the family which owns the company. Ana Schmidt is the National Sales Manager for the company in Germany and reports to Indira. She is based in Hamburg. Listen to the phone discussion between them, then answer these questions.**

a Why is Ana worried about the branding project?
b Who is her manager on that project?
c How many projects is she working on?
d Which of these does Ana identify as problems?
  1 poor communication with Indira
  2 the project leader's lack of availability
  3 failing to reach sales targets
  4 poorly defined reporting lines
  5 deteriorating work–life balance

3 **How many of the problems identified by Ana do you recognise from your own experience? What advice would you give her?**

4 **What's the best way to deal with issues like having too much work? Do you think checking or revising people's job descriptions can help?**

Focus on language 5 🎧 **14** Listen to the discussion again and identify words or expressions which mean the same as the following.

a introduced a new product into the market place

b talking to the person who your own manager reports to

c to get someone to make a decision

d an organisational structure where some employees answer to two or more managers in different departments or locations

6 Complete the sentences below about your work using the prepositions from the box.

for	in	in	on	under	with

a I work .... X (*your company*).

b I work .... the X department.

c I work .... the X sector.

d I work .... X (*the person above you in the organisation*).

e I work .... X and Y (*your colleagues*) on a daily basis.

f At the moment, I'm working .... X (*your current main project*).

7 Complete the phrases below with a word or phrase from the box, using the definitions as a guide.

allocation	gender	model	play	take on a new

a .... roles   relating to the behaviour of men and women

b .... role   assume a new responsibility

c role-...........................   an activity in which people act a situation

d role ....   giving jobs to different people

e role ....   someone who may be taken as a model to be copied

8 Complete these statements by people who are talking about their roles. The first letter(s) of each word are given.

a 'We need to cla........................... everyone's role. There's a lot of confusion.'

b 'I don't understand wh........................... does wh........................... in their department.'

c 'Roles seem to be bl........................... and ill-........................... . They need sorting out.'

d 'I think the software people should t........................... responsibility f........................... this problem and solve it.'

e 'I think we need to rev........................... our roles on a reg........................... basis.'

Let's talk 9 Role-play the continuing discussion between Indira and Ana (see Exercise 2). Spend five minutes preparing your views and ten minutes discussing the issues. After the role-play, compare the outcomes of your discussion with those of others in the group.

Ana	Indira
What solutions do you have to the general problem of lack of role clarity and with specific reference to: • workload? • stress and work–life balance? • lack of clarity within the matrix, and reporting to three different people? • your job description?	What solutions do you have to offer to the issues that Ana has raised with you?

10 What do you think should be included in a job description? Discuss with a partner, then compare your answer with the checklist in the Writing task in Section E on page 56.

B Communication skills: Negotiating

Think about it 1 What do you negotiate about at work? What do you think makes a good negotiator? Are you a good one? Can you learn to be better?

Listen to this 2  🎧 ⑮ Ana Schmidt is the National Sales Manager in Germany for an Indian food company (see Section A, Exercise 2). Following her discussion with Indira Kapoor (see Section A), she is now calling the head of the new branding project, Marie Combaluzier, in Paris. She wants to discuss the amount of time she can commit to this project. Listen to the call and match each stage in their negotiation (a–h) with the phrases that they use (1–8).

a opening – relationship building	**1** We have a deal.
b setting the agenda	**2** I'm happy with that.
c establishing the issues	**3** My proposal is …
d making a proposal	**4** I would suggest … / If you … , then I …
e bargaining	**5** How do you want to proceed? / I'd like us to …
f reaching agreement	**6** I wanted to talk about the branding project.
g summarising	**7** So to summarise, …
h closing	**8** How's the family?

3 What language would you use for each of these stages in either an informal or a formal negotiation?

4 What do you think makes this a successful negotiation?

Focus on language 5 Which of these verbs combine with *a negotiation / negotiations*?

adjourn   break off   carry out   conduct   do   enter into   make   obtain
present   put forward   renew   resume   run into   talk   work out

6 Complete the words in these sentences used at different stages in international negotiations.
   a Procedure: I'd like to begin by outl........................ our position.
   b Objectives: The main pur........................ of today's meeting is to …
   c Agenda: We have proposed four i........................ for the agenda.
   d Getting the facts straight: What t........................ are you expecting?
   e Making a counter-proposal: We'd like to make an alt........................ proposal.
   f Rejecting: I'm afraid that we're not wi........................ to do this.
   g Accepting with a condition: We can agree to this, prov........................ that you agree to our other con........................ .

7 Asking questions is an important part of negotiating. Here are some of the different kinds of question you can use. Match each type of question (a–f) with an appropriate beginning (1–6).

a	closed	1	I'm sorry, but can you explain ...?
b	open	2	What exactly do you mean by ...?
c	asking for clarification	3	Please could you elaborate on ...?
d	development	4	It's ... , isn't it?
e	small talk	5	Do you ...?
f	non-understanding	6	Could you tell me ...?

8 Complete questions 1–6 in Exercise 7. Then compare your versions with the sample answers in the key on page 108.

Let's talk **9 a** Form two teams of two, three or four Buyers and Sellers, depending on the size of the group. The teams are going to negotiate with each other as follows:

Team A (Buyers): Turn to page 93.
Team B (Sellers): Turn to page 94.

b Read your own brief, then spend 15 minutes defining your negotiating strategy. Think about the four Ps.

> **Preparation**: How can you achieve your objectives? Can you anticipate what the other side will say and how you will respond? What kind of relationship and working environment do you want to create?
> **Purpose**: What do you want to achieve? What is the least that you will accept?
> **Process**: What rules and procedures would you like to establish?
> **People**: What roles will you play, both formally (managing director, marketing director, etc.) and informally (assertive, conciliatory, etc.)?

c Meet the other side for a 25-minute negotiation.

d Debrief collectively for 15 minutes. Was the negotiation successful? How could you have done it better? Can you provide constructive feedback to individuals on their performance?

Some golden rules for negotiating successfully

DO:
- have ambitious targets, but also a fallback position.
- know the negotiating culture of your partner.
- agree roles and tactics for your negotiating team.
- establish a positive climate of collaboration when you meet.
- agree a procedure at the start.
- communicate your objectives simply and efficiently.
- listen to the other side to identify their priorities.
- be consistent.
- avoid misunderstanding and confusion by clarifying.
- respect time and try to move forward efficiently.
- reach a sustainable agreement for both parties.

DON'T:
- set unrealistic targets.
- use language which is too complex for people to understand.
- reveal all of your position too quickly.
- make assumptions about the other party's position.
- say *no* to a proposal too quickly (Avoid *Yes, but ...*)
- limit yourself with short-term thinking about short-term gain.
- lock yourself into positions.
- let yourself become bogged down in details.
- threaten the other side.
- make promises you can't keep.
- leave a negotiation without understanding the deal.

taken from *English for Negotiating Business Minimax* by Bob Dignen

As organisations become more global, more managers have to lead people over whom they have no direct authority. So managers have to spend more time trying to influence people, rather than telling them what to do.

Think about it **1** How much influencing do you do at work? And how much time do you spend telling people what to do and asking people to do things?

2 Are you good at influencing people? How do you do it?

Read this **3** David Gurteen is a consultant who runs conversational workshops called 'knowledge cafés' all over the world (see www.gurteen.com). He believes that for organisations to be successful, knowledge needs to flow in very different ways than in the past, and for this to happen, working relationships need to change. Read what he has to say.

We must stop doing things to people

Two things I often get asked are 'How do we incentivise people?' and 'How do we motivate them?'. I hear people say (or catch myself saying) 'How do we help people to see things differently?' or 'How do we support them in this change?'

Recently I have started to realise that there is a more subtle approach. Think about it. We are trying to do things to people, incentivise or motivate them; however we look at it, we are trying to change them!

David Gurteen

Notice that, in all these statements, the assumption is that we know best – that we have the right answers and others do not, and that we need to intervene and correct them.

The really important issue is that we are thinking about the world as 'us and them', when we need to be thinking in terms of 'we'.

Rather than 'I am here to help you', which implies you are in need of help and I am your saviour, we need to approach people with 'How can we work better together?'. And we need to mean that. It is not some tactic to further our own agenda. It's about approaching them without an agenda, other than to genuinely work better together.

I have also noticed another strange phenomenon. People will often tell me that the biggest excuse that their staff use for not changing, doing things differently or sharing their knowledge is that they have no time. But then the conversation moves on and when, sometime later, I ask them whether they blog, tweet, write articles or give presentations, guess what they say? 'Oh no, David. If only I had the time!' They are using exactly the same excuse.

Each year in its December issue, *Time* magazine announces its person of the year. In the December 2006 issue, in reaction to Web 2.0, it announced that person as 'you' and added 'Yes, you. You control the Information Age. Welcome to your world.'

Personally, if I had been the editor, I would have phrased it somewhat differently: 'We, yes, we. We control the information age. Welcome to our world.'

So, some thoughts for this new world:
1 Stop doing things to people.
2 Become the change we wish to see.
3 Start to work together.

We are moving to a participatory 'we' world. So whenever you initiate anything, ask yourself the question: 'Am I trying to do things to people, or am I approaching them with a genuine view to work together better?'

Focus on language   **4** **Find words or phrases in the text which mean the same as the following.**

    a encourage (people to work harder, be more productive, etc.)

    b clever and discreet

    c something we think is true, but which is not proved

    d become involved

    e suggests

    f the person who can rescue you

    g a plan to achieve an objective

    h help the progress or development of something

    i interests

    j thing

    k reason given to defend poor behaviour

    l put a scheme into operation, start something

    m sincere, honest

5 **What do you think of what David Gurteen is saying? If you think that it is interesting but it would not work in your organisation, why would it not work? What would need to change for it to work?**

6 **In their book *Communicating Internationally in English*, Bob Dignen and Ian McMaster identify eight strategies for successful influencing. They suggest eight questions to encourage us to think about what we do. Match the strategies in the box with the questions below.**

> **Be strong**　　**Be transparent**　　**Build trust**　　**Focus on the relationship**
> **Look to the future**　　**Show optimism**　　~~**Stress the benefits**~~　　**Use logical arguments**

    a Do you focus on asking people questions to find out their needs rather than telling them what you 'know' is good for them?
       Strategy: _Stress the benefits_

    b Do people know enough about you and your skills to believe in your judgement?
       Strategy: ....

    c Are you seen to be a clear communicator?
       Strategy: ....

    d Do people describe you as someone who uses logical arguments (without being too complex)?
       Strategy: ....

    e How do others view your attempts to influence them?
       Strategy: ....

    f Do others see the way you argue and persuade as being assertive or aggressive?
       Strategy: ....

    g Do others see you as inspirational and visionary?
       Strategy: ....

    h Do others see you as a positive or negative person?
       Strategy: ....

Let's talk   **7** **Work in groups of three on an influencing exercise. Once you have completed the exercise, swap roles and repeat it.**

    Student A:　Turn to page 94.

    Student B:　Turn to page 96.

    Student C:　Turn to page 90.

D Intercultural competence: Skills for working internationally

1 **What makes a good international manager? Discuss what competences and behaviours people need for successful international working.**

2 **The HR consultancy Worldwork, based in London, has created a tool called The International Profiler (TIP), which identifies a set of competences and behaviours which are important when working internationally. As you read through the list below, use this scale to assess how far you pay attention to each one when you deal with people from cultures (national, corporate, professional, ...) different from your own.**

In my intercultural working:

0 I have never thought of this as an important skill.

1 I place little focus on this / I am not very good at this.

2 I place some focus on this / I have some competence in this area.

3 I have a good focus on this / I am quite good at this.

4 I place a lot of focus on this / I am very competent in this area.

5 I do this automatically / I encourage and teach others to exercise this competence.

OPENNESS
- **New thinking**: like to be exposed to unfamiliar ideas and approaches.
- **Welcoming strangers**: keen to initiate contact and build relationships with new people.
- **Acceptance**: tolerate behaviour that is very different from their own.

FLEXIBILITY
- **Flexible behaviour**: can adapt to different cultural situations.
- **Flexible judgement**: avoid coming to quick and definitive conclusions about new people.
- **Learning languages**: motivated to learn and use the languages of business contacts.

PERSONAL AUTONOMY
- **Inner purpose**: hold strong personal values and beliefs that provide consistency when dealing with unfamiliar circumstances.
- **Focus on goals**: strong persistence in achieving goals regardless of pressures to compromise.

EMOTIONAL STRENGTH
- **Resilience**: tough enough to risk making mistakes as a way of learning; tend to 'bounce back' when things go wrong.
- **Coping**: can deal with change and pressure even in unfamiliar situations; stay calm under pressure.
- **Spirit of adventure**: ready to seek out variety, change and stimulation in life.

PERCEPTIVENESS
- **Attuned**: can focus on picking up meaning from indirect signals such as intonation, eye contact and body language.
- **Reflected awareness**: are conscious of how they come across to others.

LISTENING ORIENTATION
- **Active listening**: check and clarify, rather than assume understanding of others.

TRANSPARENCY
- **Clarity of communication**: are conscious of the need for a style that minimises the potential for misunderstandings.
- **Exposing intentions**: are able to build trust in an international context by putting needs into a clear and explicit context.

CULTURAL KNOWLEDGE
- **Information gathering**: take time to learn about unfamiliar cultures.
- **Valuing differences**: like to work with colleagues and partners from diverse backgrounds.

INFLUENCING
- **Rapport**: exhibit warmth and attentiveness when building relationships in a variety of contexts.
- **Range of styles**: can adapt style to make international partners feel comfortable.
- **Sensitivity to context**: good at understanding where political power lies in organisations.

SYNERGY
- **Creating new alternatives**: have an approach to team work that ensures that different cultural perspectives are understood and used.

adapted from *Worldwork* and *The International Profiler*

3 Discuss your profile with a partner and compare your competences and behaviours. What can you learn from your partner or from other people in the group?

Case study: Meeting the new team

Background   Michael Kahn is a German IT engineer in his early 30s. Since he left university, he has worked in the IT department of a German bank and was appointed to his first management position two years ago. At the same time, the German bank bought a retail bank in Russia. Three months ago, Michael was appointed to a team leadership post in the Russian subsidiary's head office in Moscow. His job is to work on the implementation of part of the German bank's software across all the Russian bank's branches. He has moved to Moscow with his wife and two young children.

Situation   Michael has met the members of his new team, but feels frustrated about the lack of progress he feels they are making. The eight people he manages are all software engineers aged between 25 and 60. Four are Russian, and the other four are from other parts of the former USSR. Their level of English varies significantly and also their willingness to adapt to Michael's very collaborative leadership style.

The older team members seem to expect to be told what to do all the time, but are not very clear about which part of the project they should be working on. Role allocation remains unclear to Michael, even though he has tried to find out who is supposed to be doing what. No one has a job description, and the HR manager seems to be too busy to advise or help very much.

The team is expected to fulfil ambitious targets, but the level of commitment among the engineers seems quite low, and there is some unhappiness about the amount of work that there is to do.

Task   You are senior directors in the German bank. Discuss in pairs or small groups what you think Michael should do, and draw up a time plan with milestones for its implementation. Think about which competences and behaviours identified by The International Profiler Michael should focus on, in order to get better results. Then compare your proposal with those of other groups.

E Language reference

Glossary

incentivise	to provide incentives for someone, to motivate
participatory (or participative)	an environment where everyone takes part on fairly equal terms
social tools	Examples of social tools are Facebook, LinkedIn and Twitter. Social tools together are referred to as 'the social media'.

Language summary

Prepositions following *work*

work around a problem

work for a company

work in an office

work on a project / a problem

work out in a gym (to get fit)

work through a difficult period

work to a deadline

work under a hierarchical superior
  in an organisation

work with colleagues

Stages in negotiation

A Preparation

B Meeting:
  1 Opening (relationship building)
  2 Setting the agenda
  3 Establishing the issues
  4 Making a proposal
  5 Bargaining
  6 Reaching agreement
  7 Summarising
  8 Closing

C Implementation

Language learning tips

Listening

Good listeners:

1 listen to the general subject. They don't try to understand every word and don't stop listening if they hear a word they don't know.

2 make guesses about what they are listening to, based on their knowledge of the subject, the tone of voice of the speaker, their facial expressions, body language, etc.

3 play back recordings of difficult listenings several times to try and increase understanding.

4 watch video with and then without subtitles.

5 first read the news in English, then watch the news on the TV or Internet so they are familiar with the subjects being treated.

6 note down key words and then look them up in their English–English dictionary.

7 organise regular listening practices.

Writing task

Job descriptions may include treatment of:

- the place of the job holder in the organisation
- the communication network
- information needed for the job, information to be produced, people who should see this information
- monitoring and reporting
- decision-making: what can be decided by whom
- financial budgeting and control
- producing things: what, how much and by when
- quality maintenance and how this is measured
- quality control
- innovation: expectations, how far this is expected and in what areas
- self-development: opportunities for career and promotion

Write a job description for your own ideal job.

F Tips for defining roles

1 Take a few minutes to reflect on these three tips linked to the theme of this unit. How far do you agree with each one? Which do you think is most important, and which ideas are most useful?

TIP 1

In an orchestra, roles are very clear: violinists play the violin, and trumpeters play the trumpet. In a football team, the same is true: strikers practise doing what they do best – scoring goals – and goalkeepers practise stopping them. Changing roles would not lead to successful outcomes. Good leaders are good at knowing people's strengths and encouraging them to play to those strengths, rather than focusing on their weaknesses.

Idea to help you define roles and develop your people:

● Encourage them to work on their strengths in the short term and to adopt a longer-term approach to working on their weaknesses.

TIP 2

It is not always essential to define roles clearly, but good managers recognise when it is important to do so.

Ideas to help you know when to define roles clearly:

You should clarify roles when ...

● work is unevenly distributed;
● team members are overloaded;
● people are unclear about who should do what;
● there is tension between team members.

TIP 3

Use the four Ps (preparation, purpose, process and people) to help you negotiate better.

Ideas to help you negotiate successfully:

● **Preparation**: spend as much time as you can on this. Anticipating every possible argument that the other side may come up with will help you respond faster and more effectively during the negotiation itself.
● **Purpose**: be clear about your objectives – what you would like to achieve and the least that you will accept.
● **Process**: you must all agree about rules and procedures.
● **People**: you must also define roles. Will you have someone on your side who plays a tougher role and someone who has a softer approach?

---

2 What other ideas for defining roles have you got from studying this unit?

Personal action plan **3** Think about what you have learned from this unit. Note down two or three important points which you want to apply to your own job (*What?*). Then create a schedule to implement your learning (*When?*) and think about the best way to check that you have successfully carried out your action (*How?*).

4 Discuss your personal action plan and adapt it if necessary, based on any useful feedback you get.

6 Providing support

As managers, when we fail to develop or improve the performance of our employees, we fail in our jobs.

Neil Atkinson, Director, Deminos HR, UK

AIMS

A To develop coaching skills in English
B To improve active listening skills
C To compare coaching and mentoring
D To consider different cultural attitudes to time

A Discussion and listening

Think about it

1 As a manager, how much time do you spend:

  a telling people what to do?

  b asking them to do things?

  c asking what they think would be the best way to do something?

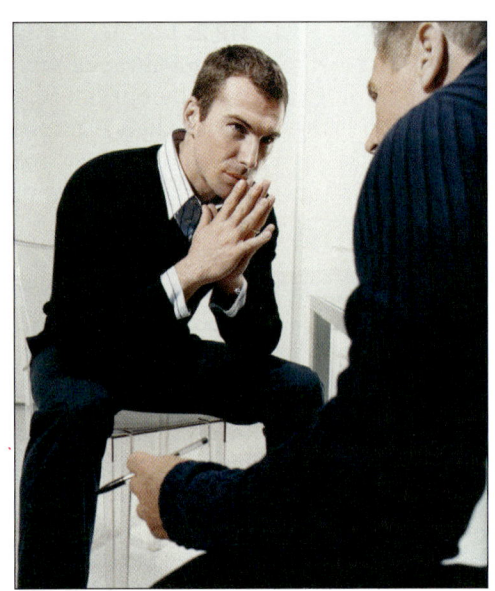

2 What are the different ways in which leaders can support the people who report to them?

3 Do you have any experience of coaching? Can you provide any examples of good or bad coaching?

Listen to this

4 🎧 **16** Tanja Keller is an HR manager for a German cement company based in Frankfurt, with responsibility for eastern and central Europe. Alex Yeshov is the HR manager of the company's Russian subsidiary, based in St Petersburg. Tanja is keen to develop her local HR leaders, so she makes a coaching call to each national manager every six weeks. Listen to the conversation between Tanja and Alex. What are the five questions that she invites Alex to ask himself during the coaching session?

5 🎧 **16** Listen again and complete these questions or statements from Tanja with between one and five words in each gap.

  a What's the .... ?

  b And what .... do you want to get from this session?

  c What's the .... ?

  d What do you need .... ?

  e .... you didn't have any interruptions at all.

  f How much time .... ?

  g Can I .... this for you?

  h Let's .... what we've got so far.

Focus on language **6** Tanja uses the four-stage GROW coaching model to frame the coaching session.

G Goal **R** Reality **O** Options **W** Win (or Will)

a Match the four letters (G, R, O, W) with these guidelines (a–d) for coaches and coachees (those who are being coached).

a Once you know where you are and where you want to go, the next step is to explore what choices you have for getting there.

b Here, the coach's intention is to gain commitment to action. Coach and coachee select the most appropriate options, commit to action, define the action plan, the next steps and a time frame for their objectives and identify how to overcome obstacles.

c As well as knowing where you are trying to get to, you need to know where you are starting from. This can often be the key part of a coaching session, and by clarifying the situation, the resolution becomes obvious and straightforward.

d The outcome should be as specific as possible and it must be possible to measure whether it has been achieved.

source: Neil Atkinson, Deminos newsletter number 34, www.deminos.co.uk

b Which do you think is the most challenging stage for a) the coach, and b) the coachee to work through?

7 a Good coaches never stop developing the ability to ask the right questions. Match each of the four letters (G, R, O, W) with these four sets of coaching questions (a–d).

a What do you want to talk about?
What have you done about this so far?

b What could you do to change the situation?
What alternatives are there to that approach?

c What will you commit to doing?
What are your next steps?
When are you going to start?

d What would you like to achieve?
Is your objective realistic?

b What other useful questions can you think of to ask at each stage in the GROW coaching process?

8 Five key coaching skills are:

a Establishing the relationship

b Questioning

c Listening

d Encouraging

e Challenging

a Match each of these skills (a–e) with the set of phrases (1–5) which best describes it.

1 praising, complimenting, celebrating success

2 provoking, asserting, speaking directly

3 building rapport, establishing trust

4 focusing on what the coachee is saying, summarising, paraphrasing

5 probing, encouraging reflection, leading to insights

b How good do you think you are at each of these skills? How do you exercise each one? Discuss and compare your coaching profile with a partner.

Let's talk **9** Role-play in pairs the rest of the coaching session between Tanja and Alex. Compare the outcome of your session with those of other pairs.

10 Using the information about coaching in this unit, take part in a coaching session with another member of your group. Take turns to coach each other for ten minutes, using the GROW model. Spend five minutes after each session evaluating its success.

B Communication skills: Active listening

1 Why is listening important for leaders?

2 How good a listener are you? Rate yourself on a scale of 1 to 5, where 5 is 'excellent'. Give reasons for your rating.

This is the only way they'll listen to me

www.CartoonStock.com

3 a 🎧 **17** Listen to the first part of an interview with Sachi Balaji, a management consultant and executive coach working in Bangalore, India. Tick (✓) the four good reasons for listening that she talks about.

    a To get the information we need to complete a task ☐

    b To understand how to influence others ☐

    c To empathise with the person you are listening to ☐

    d To assess their competence and trustworthiness ☐

    e To understand the way the other person thinks ☐

    f To show respect and to build rapport ☐

    g To hear if our ideas are understood and valued ☐

    h To monitor the speaker's style, in order to achieve better communication ☐

b Do you use all these reasons for listening? Which ones do you use most often?

4 a In the next part of the interview, Sachi is going to talk about the return on investment (ROI) or benefits to be gained from good listening. Match the words/phrases from column A with those from column B to make a list of benefits.

A	B
a better	1 costs
b more	2 mistakes
c higher	3 customers
d increased	4 relationships at work
e improved	5 productivity
f more efficient	6 creativity
g fewer	7 quality
h lower	8 motivated staff
i happier	9 information flow

b 🎧 **18** Listen and compare your answers with what Sachi says.

5 a 🎧 **18** Listen to the second part of the interview again. What are Sachi's three kinds of listener?

    a ....-focused

    b ....-orientated

    c ....-orientated

b Which kind of listener are you?

6 🎧 **19** Listen to the final part of the interview. According to Sachi, what are Covey's five levels of listening? At which level do you usually listen at work?

Focus on language **7** In their book *Communicating Internationally in English*, Bob Dignen and Ian McMaster propose a number of ways to become a better listener. Match the two halves of each of these sentences.

a	Empty your mind	**1**	feedback.
b	Support the start of a conversation	**2**	what is said.
c	Give others time	**3**	by asking questions.
d	Respond to and clarify	**4**	to end the conversation.
e	Give positive feedback,	**5**	both verbal and non-verbal.
f	Develop conversations	**6**	of your own thoughts.
g	Give yourself	**7**	by encouraging others to talk.
h	Know when to stop listening and	**8**	to say what they want to say.

8 Here are some examples of different things that active listeners say to maintain communication. Put the words in the right order to make sentences and questions.

    a to build rapport

    first / in / time / Tokyo / your / Is / this / ?

    b to develop a conversation

    lot / Japanese / have / you / a / working / people / of / experience / of / Do / with / ?

    c to empathise

    you / about / interesting / companies / what / say / It's / Mexican / .

    d to clarify information

    this / will / saying / you / your / do / that / Are / company / ?

    e to influence

    it's / experience, / to / this / mind / my / very / In / important / bear / in / .

    f to close positively

    the / with / Good / project / luck / .

Let's talk **9 a** Practise your listening skills and get feedback on your performance as a listener. Work in groups of three: one speaker, one listener and one observer to give feedback.

- Each speaker speaks for two minutes on any topic.
- The listener then summarises what the speaker said, without asking any questions or taking notes.
- The observer then comments on how successful the listener's account was.

b Now change roles and repeat the activity.

C Professional skills: Coaching and mentoring

Think about it **1** In addition to coaching, in what other ways can managers support their staff?

2 Is your team performing better than a year ago? What did you (not) do?

3 What is a mentor? What do you think are the main differences between a coach and a mentor?

Read this **4** Read this article about the differences between mentoring and coaching.

Coaching and mentoring

Coaching and mentoring use the same skills and approach, but coaching is short-term and task-based, while mentoring looks at the development of the individual in the longer term.

What is coaching?
The UK's Chartered Institute of Personnel and Development (CIPD) lists some characteristics of coaching in organisations that are generally agreed on by most coaching professionals:
- It is aimed at specific issues/areas.
- It is a relatively short-term activity.
- It is essentially a guided form of development.
- It focuses on improving performance and developing/enhancing individuals' skills.
- It can be used to address a wide range of issues.
- Coaching activities can have both organisational and individual goals.
- It works on the basis that clients are self-aware, or can achieve self-awareness.
- It is a skilled activity.
- Personal issues may be discussed, but the emphasis is on performance at work.

The core of coaching is building rapport, asking questions which lead coachees to understand themselves and their situations better, and setting goals.

Differences between mentoring and coaching
The CIPD differentiates between coaching and mentoring. Although many of the processes are similar, it is helpful to understand these differences.

mentoring	coaching
Ongoing relationship that can last for a long period of time.	Relationship generally has a fixed duration.
Can be more informal and meetings can take place as and when the 'mentee' needs some advice, guidance or support.	Generally more structured in nature and meetings are scheduled on a regular basis.
More long term and takes a broader view of the person.	Short term and focused on specific development areas/issues.
Mentor is usually more experienced and qualified than the mentee; often a senior person in the organisation who can pass on knowledge, experience and open doors to otherwise out-of-reach opportunities.	The coach doesn't usually need to have direct experience of their client's occupational role, unless the coaching is specific and skills-focused.
Focus is on career and personal development.	Focus is generally on development / issues at work.
Agenda is set by the mentee, with the mentor providing support and guidance to prepare them for future roles.	The agenda is focused on achieving specific, immediate goals.

Having done the Mentoring Skills Questionnaire, I think I need a mentor to mentor me in improving my mentoring.

www.CartoonStock.com

5 Without consulting the text, say whether these statements about coaching are true (T) or false (F) according to the author.

Coaching:

a is aimed at specific issues/areas.

b is a relatively long-term activity.

c focuses on improving performance and developing individuals' skills.

d works on the basis that clients are self-aware, or can achieve self-awareness.

e does not require any particular skill.

f puts the emphasis on performance on work.

6 Are these statements more typically made by a coachee or a mentee?

a 'We have a session for an hour every month.'

b 'We meet once every two or three months.'

c 'We've been working together for three years.'

d 'We've agreed to work together for six months.'

e 'I come away from our sessions with a better understanding of where I'm going.'

f 'I come away from our sessions with specific objectives to concentrate on.'

7 Does mentoring happen in your organisation? How do people choose a mentor?

Focus on language **8 a** A manager is reflecting on different aspects of her job. Complete each of her sentences below (a–i) with the correct form of a verb from the box.

arbitrate	consult	delegate	empower	mediate	reward

a I .... people with bonuses on the basis of their performance.

b I .... with our employee representatives on a range of issues to do with pay and working conditions.

c For less experienced members of my department, I .... tasks, but retain the final responsibility for their having been carried out.

d As far as possible, I am keen to .... the people who report to me and to encourage them to take on more responsibility.

e Occasionally, I have to .... between people when there is a conflict.

f If this doesn't work, then I ask an independent outside body to .... in any particular case.

b Which of these statements are true of your own management and leadership roles?

Let's talk **9** In their book *First Break All the Rules*, Marcus Buckingham and Curt Coffman argue that there are 12 key questions that every employee and manager should ask, in order to promote both individual employee satisfaction and good team working.

1 Do you know what is expected of you at work?

2 Do you have the resources to do your work well?

3 Do you have the opportunity to do what you do best every day?

4 Have you received recognition or praise for doing good work in the last week?

5 Does your boss care about you as a person?

6 Is there someone who encourages your development?

7 Do your opinions seem to count?

8 Does the mission/purpose of your company make you feel your job is important?

9 Are your colleagues committed to quality work?

10 Do you have a best friend at work?

11 Has someone talked to you about your progress in the last six months?

12 Have you had opportunities to learn and grow in the last year?

Consider these questions on your own, then compare your answers with a partner.
Do you have similar answers? Where there are weaknesses, what can you do to improve the situation?

D Intercultural competence: Attitudes to time

1 What five items would you place in a time capsule to represent your national culture for a future generation to discover? (Your time capsule can be quite big!)

2 a How would you describe the way you manage time?

   a Do you tend to be punctual or unpunctual?

   b Do you prefer to concentrate on one thing at a time, or are you happy dealing with several things at once?

b Compare your answers with a partner.

Read this **3** Christopher James has developed a set of learning materials for the personal and professional development of staff in his company. Read what he says about how time is viewed by different cultures.

Christopher James

Perception of time

Time is not something objective – it is relative! The perception of time changes according to the country. It has significant impact on the focus of managers, on the way managers organise themselves, and on the type of relationships the managers develop.

In *polychronic cultures* (generally Mediterranean, Middle Eastern, Asian, African, Latin American), time is flexible and approximate. Several tasks or activities can be undertaken at the same time. Interruptions are considered normal and are even expected. The development of personal relations has more importance than keeping to a pre-determined schedule. Changes are frequent, normal and considered as necessary expressions of adaptability.

For outsiders, polychronic cultures can sometimes appear to be disorganised, individualistic, talkative and unpredictable.

In *monochronic cultures* (generally German, Scandinavian, Anglo-Saxon, Northern European), time is structured and precise. Punctuality is valued. Activities are planned, and there is a tendency to concentrate on one subject at a time. Interruptions are problematic, and respecting schedules is considered important. Last-minute changes are viewed with disapproval and distrust.

For outsiders, monochronic cultures can appear to be rigid, impersonal, 'rule-driven' and inflexible.

The differences can be summarised like this:

polychronic	monochronic
1 Does many things at once.	1 Does one thing at a time.
2 Open to what is happening in the business environment.	2 Concentrates on the job, considers the environment a distraction.
3 Deadlines are an ideal, a guideline.	3 Deadlines are fixed, 'the law'.
4 Committed to people and relationships.	4 Committed to the task.
5 People are more important than process.	5 The process has its own rules .
6 Plans change often and easily.	6 Plans are followed to the letter.
7 More concerned with close relations than privacy.	7 Concerned about not disturbing other's privacy.
8 Punctuality is based on the relationship.	8 Punctuality is an end in itself.
9 Tendency to build long-lasting work relationships.	9 Accustomed to short-term relationships.
10 Works any hours.	10 Works fixed hours.

Understanding the other person's perception of time in their cultural environment will help you avoid unnecessary frustration when you work together.

4 How far do you think your country has / your company has / you have a polychronic view of time? Indicate the positions on the scale below and discuss with a colleague.

monochronic | 5 4 3 2 1 0 1 2 3 4 5 | polychronic

5 Do you have any experience of dealing with someone with a very different view of time from your own? How did you react in this kind of situation?

Case study: Creating a common culture

Background Michael works for a major international supermarket chain. He has been asked to head a group which will study the feasibility of extending the company's activities into South America. There are 12 people in the project team, three of whom are outside consultants. They all represent different functions – sales, marketing, IT, logistics, HR, etc. – and most come from and work in different countries.

Situation When Michael brought the group together for the first time for a day-long meeting to kick off the project, it didn't go well. Michael found it almost impossible to build any sense of a new team and a common purpose in the meeting room. Afterwards, he wrote some notes to try and understand the problems.

- **Punctuality**
  Half of the team arrived late - up to 20 minutes late, in fact.
  I thought it was really rude.

- **Presence**
  Some of them kept wandering in and out of the room during the meeting, especially when they were answering their phones.

- **Attention**
  At least half of them had their laptops on throughout the meeting and seemed to be paying much more attention to that.

- **Lunch and breaks**
  The breaks went on for much longer than scheduled, and when I suggested 45 minutes for lunch, they decided that they needed an hour and a half.

- **Participation**
  When people did get involved, some would start interrupting each other, and two had their own separate conversation going on for most of the day in their own language. On the other hand, three others hardly opened their mouths. One looked too frightened to speak, but the other two looked like they would have liked to say something if they'd been given a chance.

- **Leadership**
  I'm supposed to be chairing these meetings, but when I suggested switching off phones and laptops, they seemed to think I was joking.

Task Discuss with your partner: What must Michael do to ensure that the next meeting he arranges is more successful than this one?

E Language reference

Glossary

coachee	someone who is coached
competence	a skill or ability to do something
enhancing	improving
expertise	expert knowledge or skill in a particular field
non-directive	A non-directive coach minimises the guidance and direction provided to the coachee so that (s)he can find direction and answers to problems for him/herself.
premise	basis, assumption (something you assume)
rapport	Having good *rapport* with someone means having a good relationship and a good understanding with them, and getting on well with them.
respect	the admiration you feel for someone based on their abilities, qualities or achievements
time-bounded	having a clearly defined time limit
trustworthiness	the quality of deserving the trust of other people

Language summary

The GROW model for coaching

G Goal
R Reality
O Options
W Win (or Will)

Five key coaching skills

Establishing the relationship
Questioning
Listening
Encouraging
Challenging

Verbs for management and leadership

arbitrate	empower
conciliate	engage
consult	mediate
delegate	motivate
employ	reward

Language learning tips

Learning vocabulary

How many words can you learn? Three new words a day gives you more than 1,000 words in a year! Learning word combinations – words which typically go with each other – is also important. By learning typical word associations, you will increase your understanding and your ability to use the language.

How do you remember words? Some people:

- like to learn words by heart. They go through their vocabulary notebook again and again, memorising the words they have written down.
- like to read a lot. They gradually learn the meanings of words as they meet them again and again in their reading.
- associate words with particular images or sounds or smells, then remember the words through the association.
- look at the word's etymology: its origins and history.
- make links between new words and words they know in other languages.
- take each group of new words and put them all into a story.

Consider which techniques you use and which suit you best.

Writing task

First break all the rules

Following the *Let's talk* activity in Section C (Exercise 9), write down an action plan of two or three things which will help you strengthen some of the areas of team management and employee satisfaction identified by Buckingham and Coffman.

F Tips for providing support

1 Take a few minutes to reflect on these six tips for coaches. How far do you agree with each one? Which do you think is most important, and which ideas are most useful?

TIP 1

Zip it. You may feel tempted to provide your coachee with your answers, but you should resist it. Aim for 70–80% coachee talking time. By finding the answers from within themselves, coachees are more likely to engage with the solution they identify and to work towards realising it.

TIP 2

Encourage silence. You both need time to think. Pause before asking your question if you need to. Encourage your coachee to think before answering.

TIP 3

The problem that the coachee starts with may not be the same as the one you finish with. Don't be afraid to help the coachee to redefine the problem.

TIP 4

You can be a workplace coach to help your people deal with workplace issues, but you are probably not a qualified counsellor, psychologist or psychotherapist. Be very aware of the line between workplace coaching and other more personal areas, and don't overstep it.

TIP 5

Explore other types of coaching:
- self-coaching
- team coaching
- peer coaching
- co-coaching

TIP 6

Some coaches ask their coaches to fill in a short form like the one below before a coaching session.

Coaching preparation form

Preparing for the coaching session will allow you to optimise your results and our coaching time together. Please e-mail this to me before the session. Write as little or as much as you like! Remember – you set the agenda.

1 How am I, today, right now?
2 How has my week been?
3 What do I want to get out of the session today?
4 What actions did I take since our last session? What were my accomplishments last week?
5 What were the main things I would have liked to have achieved but didn't?
6 What issues am I facing right now?

---

2 Answer the questions in Tip 6 quickly, then present the contents to your partner.

Personal action plan 3 Think about what you have learned from this unit. Note down two or three important points which you want to apply to your own job (*What?*). Then create a schedule to implement your learning (*When?*) and think about the best way to check that you have successfully carried out your action (*How?*).

4 Discuss your personal action plan and adapt it if necessary, based on any useful feedback you get.

7 Giving and receiving feedback

*I have yet to find the man who did not do better work and put forth greater
effort under a spirit of approval than under a spirit of criticism.*

Charles Schwab, US businessman

AIMS

A To give and receive better feedback
B To improve effectiveness in meetings
C To develop ways of dealing with underperformance
D To consider the impact of culture on feedback

A Discussion and listening

Think about it
1 What is feedback? What is the best feedback you have ever a) given, and b) received?

Listen to this
2 a 🎧 **20–23** John, Elsi, Kenji and Nick work with Céline in the busy London office of an international company. After a meeting she had chaired, Céline asked each of them for feedback on her performance. Listen to their reactions and match each of these descriptions (a–d) to the correct speaker (1–4).

Giving feedback is a complex process.

www.CartoonStock.com

a negative feedback	1 John
b constructive feedback	2 Elsi
c praise	3 Kenji
d positive feedback	4 Nick

b Based on what you have heard, how do you define the differences between these four different types of response?

3 Which of the responses in Exercise 2 would you most like to hear in relation to your own performance? Which do you think is the most useful to Céline?

4 a 🎧 **24** Listen to Nick giving Céline some more feedback after another presentation she made. As you listen, number the steps below in Nick's feedback in the order in which he gives it.

a Start with something positive but specific. ☐
b Provide feedback which helps the person to do better next time. ☐
c Give praise (if praise is deserved). ☐
d Give a reason for this feedback. ☐
e Ask the person what they thought of their own performance. ☐
f Get feedback on your feedback. ☐
g Give a reason for this feedback. ☐

b What do you think of Nick's approach to giving feedback? Would you use the same approach?

Focus on language

5 a Complete each of the expressions of praise and thanks below (a–j) with a word from the box.

> appreciate   contribution   efforts   excellent
> helpful   job   piece   step   well   work

  a .... done.
  b Bravo. You did a good ....
  c Thanks a lot for all your ....
  d That's really ....
  e I really .... it.
  f You made an important ....
  g That's very good ....
  h This is a very good .... of work.
  i This is a big .... forward.
  j Congratulations – an .... performance!

b Can you add any other useful expressions to this list?

6 a Match the two halves of this advice about giving feedback.

  a The objective of feedback is to   1 praise and feedback.
  b Get feedback first, because then   2 a feedback culture.
  c We should distinguish between   3 feedback is multi-directional.
  d You give negative feedback only   4 help the other person to do better
  e In high-performing teams,   next time.
  f Create   5 you can avoid repeating what the other
                                              person already knows.
                                            6 to deal with serious underperformance.

b Do you agree with this advice? How can you build a feedback culture in your team, department or organisation?

7 Complete the advice below on receiving feedback given to the managers of a major multinational with the verbs from the box.

> accept   avoid   consider   formulate   take

  a .... the feedback as information – it is the view of the person giving it.
  b .... time to .... the feedback.
  c .... arguing, denying or justifying as it prevents you from really listening.
  d Where you feel the feedback is relevant and accurate, ... a plan to address the issues raised.

Let's talk

8 How strong is the feedback culture in your organisation? Mark your answers somewhere along each line, then compare with your colleagues' and discuss them.

a I give enough feedback. ——————————————————— I don't give enough feedback.
b I receive enough feedback. ——————————————————— I don't receive enough feedback.
c I give feedback at the right time. ——————————————— I don't give feedback at the right time.
d I'm a good listener. ——————————————————————— I'm not a good listener.
e I often give praise. ——————————————————————— I never give praise.
f I always start by giving positive feedback. ————————— I never start by giving positive feedback.
g I always give reasons for the feedback I give. ————————— I never give reasons for the feedback I give.
h I always give developmental feedback. ————————————— I never give developmental feedback.
i I'm sensitive to the cultures of the people ————————— I'm not sensitive to the cultures of the
to whom I give feedback.   people to whom I give feedback.

B Communication skills: Managing meetings

Think about it **1** Tell a partner about a bad meeting that you attended recently. What would have made it better?

2 Tell a partner about a good meeting that you attended recently. What made it successful?

Listen to this **3** 🎧 **25** Tomoji Nishioka is on his first professional visit to Europe. At the moment, he is in Oslo and is asking his Norwegian colleague, Monica Bakke, about how meetings are run in her company. As you listen, choose the correct answer to these questions according to what Monica says. One of the questions has two correct answers.

a Where does the meeting take place?
1 in a meeting room
2 in a restaurant
3 in a private home

b Who can you talk to?
1 everyone
2 people below you in the hierarchy
3 anyone who has spoken to you

c What do people talk about during the meeting?
1 business matters only
2 social matters first, then business
3 business matters first, then social

d When can you speak?
1 when the chair allows you to
2 at any time
3 when another speaker has finished speaking

e How much do you say?
1 as much as you like
2 as little as possible
3 as much as you need to make your point, but no more

f When are the real decisions made?
1 before the meeting
2 during the meeting
3 after the meeting

g When do meetings start?
1 on time
2 10 minutes after the scheduled time
3 20 minutes after the scheduled time

4 What are the answers to the questions in Exercise 3 for your organisation? Is there anything you would like to change about the way that meetings are run?

5 In some organisations, people spend five minutes at the end of every meeting discussing how it went and how it might be managed better next time. Would this be useful in your organisation?

6 Replace the verbs in bold below with the correct form of another verb from the box with the same or a similar meaning.

> arrange   cancel   chair   get to   hold
> postpone   reschedule   take part

a Originally, the meeting was **fixed** for Monday morning at nine o'clock.

b But Gill couldn't **make** it then, and she had to be there to **run** it.

c So it was **rearranged** for Tuesday at midday.

d That was no good for Fritz, so it was **put back** again to Wednesday.

e Then Suzanne said she would only be able to **participate** until three.

f We thought of **calling** it **off** altogether.

g Finally, we're **having** the meeting on Friday afternoon at five o'clock.

7 a Match each of the meetings expressions below (1–6) to a stage in the opening part of a meeting (a–f).

a Introduce newcomers to the others, if necessary.

b Offer apologies for absence from those unable to attend.

c Define the objectives of the meeting.

d Introduce the agenda.

e Allocate roles to the participants.

f Agree on timings for each item and for the duration of the meeting.

1 I'd like to spend no more than 20 minutes on each point and I hope we'll be finished by three. OK?

2 We have four main items to discuss.

3 I'd like Adrian to lead on the first point and Suzanne to make a short presentation when we get to item 3.

4 I don't think you all know Ann-Marie. She has just joined us from head office.

5 Now, the reason we're all here today is to decide the future of the Atlas project.

6 Kurt and Antonio are sorry not to be able to attend today.

b Can you suggest any other expressions for each step (a–f)?

8 Complete these phrases (a–j) with the correct set of verbs and adjectives (1–10).

a to .... a suggestion ☑
b a .... suggestion ☐
c to .... a decision ☐
d a .... decision ☐
e to .... a plan ☐

f a .... plan ☐
g to .... an objective ☐
h a(n) .... objective ☐
i to .... an opinion ☐
j a(n) .... opinion ☐

1 detailed / ingenious / contingency / short-term

2 achieve / meet / set / state / agree / formulate

3 unanimous / joint / final / wise / fair / hasty / poor / quick

4 take / come to / take / reach / reconsider

5 personal / expert / honest / strong / objective / positive

6 primary / secondary / main / major / realistic / long-term / ultimate

7 good / constructive / helpful / ridiculous / useful

8 present / approve / reject / carry out / drop / implement

9 make / put forward / invite / welcome / reject

10 have / hold / express / give / ask for / agree with

9 Form groups of (ideally) five or six and organise a troubleshooting meeting. Appoint an observer to give you feedback at the end of the meeting.

Observer: Turn to page 90.
Participants: Turn to page 95.

Think about it 1 'Negative feedback is only useful or justified in cases of underperformance.' Do you agree with this?

2 What do you think is the best way to deal with people whose work is below standard?

Read this 3 Read these management guidelines on how to deal with poor performance. As you read, think about whether you find this approach helpful. How does it compare with what you do in cases of underperformance?

Does anyone else have any complaints?

Performance gap analysis

Do you have a performance problem in your team?
Do you wish to find the most appropriate response?

The Gap Analysis Method can help you. It presents 15 key questions, in a given order.
They will help you identify the fundamental causes of the problem.

1 **Who is not doing what is expected?**
Identify the job role of the person involved.
2 **What is the performance discrepancy?**
Find the difference between what is being done, and what should be done.
Identify the event that revealed the discrepancy.
3 **What is the cost of the performance discrepancy?**
4 **Are there other future repercussions?**
Identify what would happen if nothing was done about the discrepancy.
5 **Is the discrepancy important?**
Decide whether dealing with the problem would have a worthwhile result.
6 **Can we simplify the performance:**
… by establishing a more streamlined process?
… by training the person?
… by more motivating management?
7 **Is there a skills deficiency?**
Examine whether the person does perform correctly from time to time.
8 **Has the person met expectations in the past?**
See if the person has ever performed as desired.

9 **Does the person know how well they are doing?**
Is the person receiving appropriate feedback on their performance?
10 **Is the person capable of learning?**
Estimate their potential to improve performance when trained.
11 **Is the desired performance punishing?**
Will the person be at a disadvantage if they improve?
12 **Is non-performing rewarding?**
Examine why the person justifies doing it in the present way.
13 **Does performing really matter to them?**
Identify what will persuade them to perform better (pride, satisfaction, belonging …).
14 **Are there any obstacles to performing?**
Check whether the person knows exactly what is expected, in each situation.
Appreciate conflicting demands on the person's time. What other priorities are there?
15 **Which solution is the best?**
Find which solution is the easiest and quickest, requiring the least investment.

BUT REMEMBER, if the problem is:
• a lack of skills, training is a possible solution.
• a lack of motivation, better management is the solution.
• an organisational one, better processes are the solution.

4 Have you had to deal with a case of underperformance? Describe the situation briefly. What did you do? Did it work?

Focus on language **5 a** Complete each of the comments below, made by managers during interviews with underperforming employees, with a word from the box.

absent	expected	improvement	lateness
performance	productivity	standard	targets

    a 'Your .... recently has been unsatisfactory.'
    b 'Your .... is not high enough.'
    c 'Can you tell me why you have been .... from work so much recently?'
    d 'We are concerned about your frequent .... in the morning.'
    e 'You're not performing to the .... we expect and require.'
    f 'We need to agree on some performance ....'
    g 'We propose creating a performance .... plan.'
    h 'Are you clear about what is .... of you?'

b Do you think these are the right things to say to an underperforming employee? What would you say?

6 a Receiving negative feedback can be an emotional experience. Put these words for describing feelings in the correct column of the table below.

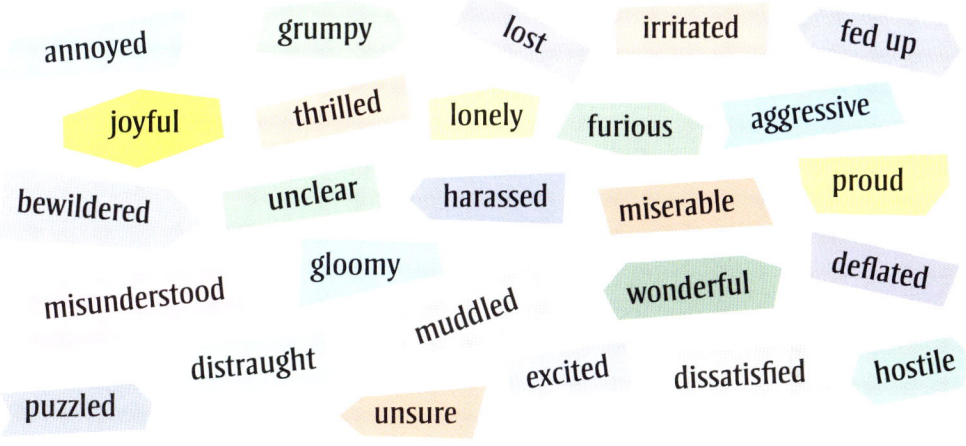

happy	sad	angry	confused

b Which of these do you feel at work at least sometimes? Compare your choices with a partner's.

Let's talk **7** Work in groups of three.

Student A: Turn to page 97.
Student B: Turn to page 95.
Student C: Turn to page 91.

When Students A and B have received feedback from Student C (the observer), you may wish to change roles and repeat the exercise.

D Intercultural competence: Feedback across cultures

1 Read this article posted by Lauren Supraner on the CAL Learning blog, then answer this question.

Do you agree with Lauren's analysis of the impact of culture on the way we give and receive feedback?

GIVING FEEDBACK ACROSS CULTURES

Task-oriented cultures and relationship-oriented cultures give and receive feedback differently. Knowing the differences between these two types of culture, and how to apply their preferred style of communicating, will make your feedback more acceptable. Always keep in mind, 'What is the most effective way to get my message across? What type of feedback will this person be most receptive to hearing?'

Feedback for task-oriented cultures: LAY IT ON THE LINE
In these cultures, such as in the US, the person and the task are viewed separately. Feedback is direct, specific and quantifiable. It is expected that the person receiving the feedback will engage in discussion, rather than sit quietly.

Feedback for relationship-oriented cultures: READ BETWEEN THE LINES
In cultures such as Asian and Hispanic, the person and task are not separated. Feedback on work is taken personally, and saving face becomes important. Direct negative feedback leads to a loss of face, and therefore performance feedback is often indirect. Calling attention to individual contributions may also be viewed negatively.

Giving feedback to non-native speakers of English
If you are giving feedback to someone who is not fluent in English, adjust your feedback accordingly. Speak in shorter sentences. Check regularly for comprehension by asking questions, avoid using idioms or jargon, and provide both spoken and written feedback. Sending a follow up e-mail summarising your feedback gives the person a chance to clarify any misunderstanding.

---

2 a Think about how people give and receive feedback in your organisation. Describe the way it is carried out, using these guidelines:

Where I work, feedback is generally more:
- positive or constructive / negative
- formal / informal
- top-down / bottom-up (or in other directions)
- frequent / infrequent
- helpful / unhelpful
- focused on the person / focused on the task
- concerned with face-saving / not concerned with face-saving
- direct / indirect

b Compare your conclusions with a partner's and with other members of the group. Which aspects of the feedback culture of your organisation would you like to change? How could this be achieved?

Case study: Cultural merger

Background Portland Sports is a successful manufacturer of climbing equipment based in Oregon, US. It has recently been bought by a fast-growing and acquisitive German sports-equipment company. There are a number of other subsidiaries in the group which have also been bought over the last five years, including a French ski manufacturer and a Canadian golf-equipment company. All three of these companies were founded 20 to 40 years ago by sports enthusiasts in their own field; all three have a strong reputation for research, product excellence and innovation; all three employ people who are passionate about their products and about the sport they practise, and all enjoy strong customer loyalty. The German parent company has a reputation for strong financial discipline and centralised control.

Situation The German parent is now reorganising the company into product categories, so that sports clothing and auxiliary equipment (bags, etc.) form one division. From now on, the local companies will work across national boundaries with each other. The President of the clothing category has called a meeting in London of representatives of all three subsidiaries, together with representatives of the parent company, to define a strategy for the future and for creating a common culture. The two-day meeting will be organised and facilitated by a firm of management consultants that the President has worked with before.

Task The task of the consultant is to design a two-day meeting for about 20 people which will achieve the objectives of the client. The consultant has therefore organised a Webex meeting for five people to plan the meeting:

1 the consultant (role A on page 97)
2 the President of the clothing division (role B on page 91)
3 a management representative from Portland Sports (role C on page 96)
4 a management representative from the French ski manufacturer (role D on page 93)
5 a management representative from the Canadian golf equipment manufacturer (role E on page 96)

Form groups of five, allocate and then read your respective roles. Then role-play the meeting.

E Language reference

Glossary

compensation	pay
discrepancy	a difference between expected and actual performance
obstacles	barriers, things that block your way
penalised	punished
repercussions	results or effects
streamlined	making a process more efficient or effective
worthwhile	something useful, interesting or rewarding enough to justify the time or money spent on it

Language summary

Language for giving thanks and praise

Well done.
Bravo! You did a good job.
Thanks a lot for all your efforts.
That's really helpful.
I really appreciate it.
You made an important contribution.
That's very good work.
This is a very good piece of work.
This is a big step forward.
Congratulations! An excellent performance

Defining a meetings culture

Where do your meetings take place?
Who can you talk to?
What do people talk about?
When can you speak?
How much do you speak?
When are the real decisions made?
Do meetings start on time?

Word combinations for meetings

to make / put forward / invite / welcome / reject **a suggestion**
a good / constructive / helpful / ridiculous / useful **suggestion**
to take / come to / take / reach / reconsider **a decision**
a unanimous / joint / final / wise / fair / hasty / poor / quick **decision**
to present / approve / reject / carry out / drop / implement **a plan**
a detailed / ingenious / contingency / short-term **plan**
to achieve / meet / set / state / agree / formulate **an objective**
a(n) primary / secondary / main / major / realistic / long-term / ultimate **objective**
to have / hold / express / give / ask for / agree with **an opinion**
a(n) personal / expert / honest / strong / objective / positive **opinion**

Language learning tips

Creating opportunities to speak English

A lot of people who want to improve their English in order to be more effective professionally lack opportunities to practise. How can you practise speaking English on a more regular basis in your personal and professional life? Consider these possibilities:

- Rather than send an e-mail in English, call the person whom you correspond with.
- There may be an English-speaking student in the town or city where you live who will exchange English conversation and conversation in your language with you.
- When English-speaking visitors come to your organisation, can you join the welcoming party? show them around? make a presentation to them? join them for lunch?
- Find someone to Skype with in English.
- Some people create an English-speaking table in their company restaurant once a week.

Brainstorm your own ideas for increasing the opportunities to practise with your colleagues.

Writing tasks

1 Think of an example of professional performance that you have seen in a colleague recently and write him or her an e-mail providing both praise for and constructive feedback on the performance.
2 Write down some guidelines for a more junior manager on how to manage underperformance in an employee.

TIP 1

A procedure for giving feedback

1 Get feedback on their performance from the person you're giving feedback to.
2 Give praise (if praise is deserved).
3 Start with something positive but specific.
4 Give a reason for this feedback.
5 Provide feedback which helps the person to do better next time.
6 Give a reason for this feedback.
7 Get feedback on your feedback.

The aim of feedback is to help the person to do better next time. Always provide takeaway value when you give feedback.

Feedback doesn't need to be negative.

www.CartoonStock.com

TIP 2

The formal annual appraisal
Formal annual appraisals should consolidate all the feedback that you have given or received regularly over the year; they should also look forward to next year, in relation both to individuals' objectives, and their professional and personal development. You shouldn't hear or say anything in an annual appraisal about someone's performance that you haven't heard or said already.

TIP 3

'Pixar plussing'
Walt Disney's great ability was to get people to do better work than they imagined they were capable of. He coined the term *plussing* as a way of making an idea even better, and he frequently told his animators to *plus* it, even when they had already produced very good work. Today at Pixar, managers have a very direct way to get feedback called *Pixar plussing*. They simply say: 'Just tell me what needs changing'.

TIP 4

SARA for managing feedback to underperformers
Recipients of challenging feedback may go through and be helped through these stages: Shock → Anger → Recognition → Acceptance. Managers can find the SARA model helpful when they have to tell a report something that the report may not want to hear. It explains the stages of Shock, Anger, Recognition and Acceptance that we can go through when we get feedback which, although it may be accurate and fair, we find very direct or difficult to accept.

8 Representing a team

Outstanding leaders go out of their way to boost the self-esteem of their personnel. If people believe in themselves, it's amazing what they can accomplish.

Sam Walton, founder of Walmart

AIMS

A To represent the team effectively
B To improve presentation skills
C To review good leadership qualities
D To celebrate success across cultures

A Discussion and listening

Think about it   **1**   Do other parts of your organisation know what your team is doing? How well is your team represented?

2   Why do you think it is important for a team to be well represented? What can happen if a team is not well represented?

Listen to this   **3**   🎧 **26**   Bill Daley is an American software engineer who works for a US bank in Moscow. He heads a mixed team of Russians and Americans. Listen to a conversation between him and Dmitri Martov, one of the young engineers in his team, then answer these questions.

   a   Where has Bill been?
   b   Why did he go?
   c   Did he succeed?
   d   Why is Dmitri angry?

4   Dmitri starts to give Bill some ideas about how he can represent the team better. What advice would you give Bill?

Focus on language **5** Complete each of the sentences below about representation with a word from the box.

> communication   competent   demotivated
> hierarchical   influencing   internally   overall   ownership
> political   recognition   'sell'   visible

a No matter how well a team is working, without wider ...., team members will become ....

b It is really important that the leader ensures that communication about what the team is doing takes place both .... and externally.

c Inside the team, members need an .... sense of how the team's work is going.

d There must be regular .... of progress both face to face (if possible) and electronically.

e Outside the team and if the organisation is not too ...., the leader may identify other team members who are .... and confident to represent the team's work to more senior management.

f This can help the team to feel greater .... of the projects they are working on.

g All teams need to be .... to the rest of the organisation.

h Team leaders and members should miss no opportunity to .... the work they are doing to the wider organisation.

i Teams need to think about which members are best at exercising both .... and .... skills outside the team. It may not be the leader.

6 a What skills do you need to ensure good representation of the team? Provide your own words to complete these statements.

a .... skills – getting your message across and changing the minds of influential people.

b .... skills – understanding how power is distributed and used within an organisation and which people have influence. This can often be difficult for people working in unfamiliar cultures.

c .... skills – it's important to be aware of whether or not the culture you are working in places more or less importance on a high level of technical competence.

d .... skills – for example, to arrange an international meeting.

e .... skills – knowing how to adapt your exercise of these other skills, according to the cultural context.

f .... skills – someone must be able to present the work of the team convincingly and attractively to the wider world.

b To what extent do you possess these different skills? Can you think of ways or situations in which you could develop them further?

Let's talk **7** Form groups of three or four and prepare a plan to communicate your team's recent achievements.

- Decide on the work that your team does. You know you do good work, but the problem is that no one else out there knows. You don't have enough exposure and, as a result, senior management has said that it wants to cut your budget by 25% next year. You have to come up with convincing reasons why this should not happen.

- Together prepare:
  - a five-minute presentation on why your budget should not be cut, which one of you will deliver to the rest of the class;
  - a plan for significantly improving the amount of exposure that your team gets in the future to avoid this problem happening again, which another member of the group will present to the rest of the class.

- The class can decide on the best presentation and best plan at the end of the activity.

Think about it **1** 'All international team members need good presentation skills.'
What are the best ideas for giving a good presentation? Work in pairs to make a list, then tell the rest of the group your top three tips for a successful presentation.

Listen to this **2** 🎧 **27** Listen to Isabelle Dutoit, a French member of an international project, talking about the team's work. When you have listened, answer these questions.

   a Who is Isabelle talking to?

   b How do we know that the team has achieved good exposure of its work?

   c Why do you think the team leader has given Isabelle the job of making this presentation?

   d Do you think that she should admit to feeling nervous?

   e What key word does Isabelle use to show that she's speaking for the whole team?

3 Which of these statements about making presentations do you agree with, and why?

- You should always say what you are going to talk about, and why.
- It's better to get on with the subject of the presentation, rather than spending time introducing yourself and your organisation.
- Effective use of your voice is more important than good visuals.
- *How* you say it is more important that *what* you say.
- The world would be a better place without PowerPoint.
- If you don't know the answer to a question, don't pretend that you do.
- In our organisation, it would be helpful if we could halve the number of presentations that we give every year, and then halve the length of the ones that we do give.

4 What do you think are your three biggest strengths and three biggest weaknesses as a presenter? Discuss these with a colleague and ask them for advice about how to deal with the areas you need to work on. Write down a short action plan based on what you have discussed.

5 Complete the words in these presentation tips.

a Learn your introduction b........................ h........................ . This helps you to overcome initial nerves and to focus on your audience.

b The first three minutes are important for getting the audience's a........................ .

c Use a 'hook' to achieve this: ask a question, tell a s........................ or show them something which they will remember.

d Signal the s........................ of your talk at the beginning and regularly throughout it.

e Don't be afraid to give particularly strong s........................ to key words.

f Be absolutely clear about the m........................ m........................ that you want your audience to take away from the talk.

g V........................ the speed at which you speak and slow down to emphasise key points.

h The g........................ rule for business presentations is: First say what you're going to say, then say it, then say what you've said.

i Don't let q........................ take over the show. Always remember that you are in charge.

j Don't try to be someone you're not. Just be y........................ .

6 Complete the key phrases for presentations below with the words and phrases in the box.

aim	attention	divided	interrupt	of all	over
point	recommendation		subject	turn	

a First .... , I'd like to thank you all for coming.

b The .... of this presentation is The Future of Web 3D.

c My .... is to survey the different standards so we can make a decision about which to adopt.

d I've .... the talk into three main parts.

e Please feel free to .... me if you have any questions or comments.

f That's all I want to say about the background, so let's .... to the second part.

g I'm sorry, perhaps that wasn't very clear. I'll go .... it again.

h This brings me to my third and final ....

i So my main .... is that we should adopt the new standard.

j Thank you for your ....

7 Prepare and deliver a short presentation on a success story of a team you have worked with or are working with now. Then ask for feedback from other group members on your presentation style. You can tell them what particular aspect(s) of your presentation you would like feedback on, or you can ask them to comment under headers like:

- overall effectiveness
- clarity of message
- organisation: opening – body – close
- level of interest of the content
- use of voice
- visuals
- audience management
- question handling

8 How do you and your team celebrate success? First tell your partner about a good team celebration that you have experienced, then brainstorm with them five or six other ways that teams can celebrate success. Round off by sharing your ideas with the rest of the group.

Read this 1 **Joseph Nye has been writing about leadership in business and politics for many years. Here is a summary of his views on leadership taken from one of his books, *The Powers to Lead*. As you read, consider this question:**

Do you think Nye's views work for leaders everywhere, or do you think they are valid only for the United States?

Joseph Nye

Leadership: A dozen quick take-aways

1 Good leadership matters. Good = effective and ethical. Luck matters for success, but good leaders can help shape their luck.

2 Almost anyone can become a leader. *Leadership can be learned*. It depends on nurture as well as on nature. Leadership can exist at any level, with or without formal authority. Most people are both leaders and followers. They 'lead from the middle'.

3 Leaders help *create and achieve group goals*. Thus effectiveness requires *both* vision and interpersonal/organisational skills.

4 Smart leaders need both *soft and hard skills*. They need to be able to exercise a *transformational* style by appealing to people's higher ideals and values; and a *transactional* style – using more traditional leadership tools like reward or punishment. One is not automatically better than the other.

5 Leaders depend on and are *partly shaped by followers*. Presence/magnetism is inherent in some personalities more than others, but *charisma* is largely bestowed by followers.

6 *Appropriate style depends on the context*. There are 'autocratic situations' and 'democratic situations', normal and crisis conditions, and routine and new crises. Good leaders can diagnose whether there is a need for change or not.

7 A *consultative style* is more costly in terms of time, but it *provides more information, creates commitment and empowers followers*.

8 Managers are not necessarily leaders, but effective leaders usually need *both managerial and organisational skills*. They create and maintain systems and institutions. Leaders are not mere deciders; they help a group decide how to decide.

9 Leadership for *crisis* conditions requires advanced preparation, emotional maturity, and the ability to distinguish the roles of *operational, analytical and political work*. The appropriate mix of styles and skills varies with the stage of the crisis.

10 The information revolution is causing a long-term shift from a command style to a more co-operative style. Network organisations require more consultation.

11 Reality testing, constant information seeking, and adjusting to change are essential for good results. *Emotional intelligence* and *practical knowledge* are more important than pure IQ in judgement.

12 Ethical leaders use their consciences, common moral rules and professional standards, but conflicting values can create complex situations that are difficult to resolve.

2 Without referring to the text, decide whether these claims are true (T) or false (F), according to Nye.

a You can learn to be a leader.

b Good leaders must also be good managers and organisers.

c Good leaders do not need vision if they have good interpersonal and organisational skills.

d Good leaders shape their followers, not the other way round.

e A command style of leadership is preferable to a consultative style because it is quicker.

f Leaders help groups decide how to decide.

g Emotional intelligence and practical knowledge are more important in a leader than IQ.

3 Discuss with your colleagues how far you agree with Nye on each of his 12 points. If you disagree, can you propose an alternative leadership 'rule'?

Focus on language **4** Managing the work–life balance of staff is becoming an increasingly important leadership skill. David Clutterbuck is a specialist who advises businesses on how to achieve a better work–life balance for employees. Here are some of the facts and ideas that David uses to talk about this subject. Complete each sentence below with a word or phrase from the box.

> business imperative   business integrity
> psychological contract   out of hours   outstrips   self-fulfilment
> resilience   social responsibility   value   well-being

a Eighty-three per cent of British managers are contacted ....

b Work–life balance is a state where an individual manages real or potential conflict between different demands on his or her time and energy in a way that satisfies their needs for .... and ....

c Six reasons for promoting work–life balance within an organisation are recruitment and retention, performance, reduced absenteeism, creativity, commitment and ....

d In Europe, work–life balance has been approached mainly from a perspective of ....

e In the US, it is mainly seen as a ....

f What does success mean to you? Success equals achieving what you ....

g Who has call on your time, mental energy, emotional energy, physical energy? If demand .... supply, what are your priorities?

h You build personal .... by:
  – remaining in touch with your personal values and priorities;
  – building an appropriate support network and being constantly on guard for signs of creeping overload in any one part of your life;
  – managing the crises in a focused manner with the support of others.

i To what extent does the .... between this organisation and its employees enable them to become the people they want to be?

5 How is your work–life balance? How is the work–life balance of your team members? Does your organisation have a policy on this?

Let's talk **6** David Clutterbuck talks about the importance of the following six areas of people's lives. In pairs, discuss how much attention you pay to each of these.

- work
- career
- domestic/family life
- health/fitness
- self-fulfilment
- spiritual/community

D Intercultural competence: Celebrating success across cultures

1 How do people celebrate success around the world? Read these responses. Which country do you think each of these quotations comes from? How do you normally celebrate success?

a 'We generally all go out for a meal together.'

b 'We go to the sauna with some beers and then jump in the lake, or if it's the winter, we roll in the snow.'

c 'We go to different bars and we all sing karaoke. The boss and the senior managers of the team always sing first and they sing most.'

d 'We pay successful individuals big bonuses and we announce their names in a team meeting with the head of the division present.'

e 'We all go round to the house of someone in the team and have a barbecue. Everyone brings some food for the meal.'

f 'We organise an away-day – generally with a team-building event in the morning and skiing or some other outdoor activity in the afternoon.'

g 'We all meet in the big hall, and the Chief Executive makes a speech to the whole staff about the good work that we've done. There are other speeches as well from other senior managers, and it makes us feel very proud.'

2 You are the leader of an international team, which has now completed a long and very challenging project – the research, design and launch of a major new product. Your people are from Asia, Europe and the US. The team met its major goals, but along the way, there were a number of problems:

- Some team members had to be replaced.
- The research budget was significantly overspent.
- The launch had to be rescheduled twice due to design and production problems.

You want to celebrate all the good work that has been done, but you also want the team to learn from the experience of what did not go so well. Decide what you will say when you talk to the team and how you will celebrate its achievements.

Case study: Case-building exercise

In pairs, you are going to work on your own short intercultural case, using the framework below.

1 Read the Background, Situation and Task below.
2 Discuss with a partner the details of the team and the kick-off event. Your objective is to achieve the best possible start to your project.
3 Prepare together a short presentation on your team and the programme for the kick-off event.
4 Deliver your joint presentation to the rest of the group and give other pairs feedback on theirs.
5 As a group, summarise the best practices for kick-off meetings of this kind from the ideas you have heard.

Background You have been appointed as joint heads of an international project team in a multinational company, which has two years to achieve its objectives. Success in this project will be very good for your careers. Team members are based in different countries all over the world.

Situation You have just started your new job. There is a budget for all team members to attend a kick-off meeting, to get the project off the ground. This meeting will take place in six weeks' time.

Task You need to plan the two-day kick-off meeting so as to ensure the best possible start to the project. What programme do you propose?

Decide on the following details for your case:
- company sector (e.g. food, telecoms, banking)
- the aim of the project
- size of team (maximum ten)
- nationalities and jobs of team members (at least five different)
- location of kick-off meeting
- objectives of kick-off meeting
- programme

Day 1

1

2

3

4

evening event

Day 2

1

2

3

4

close and departure

E Language reference

Glossary

charisma	personal qualities of an individual which can attract, influence and inspire people
hook	a curved piece of metal used, for example, to catch a fish; a way of engaging the attention of a group, for example, at the beginning of a presentation
nurture	the influence of the environment on the development of an individual
nature	the influence of inherited or innate characteristics on the development of an individual
represent	to speak or act officially on behalf of a group
resilience	the capacity of a person to recover quickly from shock, injury or difficulty

Language summary

Representing the team

Teams need wider **visibility**. Teams need **recognition** to maintain **motivation** and **commitment**. They need someone to ensure that the outside world knows what they are doing, also to **ensure** adequate **budget and resources** for their work. Internally, teams need good **communication** so people know what their colleagues are doing. Recounting **success stories** and **celebrating success** help with this process. Representation needs even more careful thought when the team is **virtual** or **international**, working on a **project**, or part of a **matrix** organisation, or any combination of these.

Useful language for presentations

I'd like to thank you all for coming.
The subject of this presentation is …
My aim is to …
I've divided the talk into three main parts.
Please feel free to interrupt me if you have any questions or comments.
Let's turn to the second part.
Sorry, I'll go over that again.
This brings me to my third and final point.
So my main recommendation is that …
Thank you for your attention.

Language learning tips

- Be active. Learning is an active process. Think about what happens when you learn something. How did it happen? Think of different ways of achieving the same learning targets.
- Be realistic. There are no magic solutions.
- Take the time to learn. But set deadlines.
- Be patient.
- Be positive. Even when you think you're not making progress, you probably are.
- Use technology. New technology gives you access to language in many different forms.
- Use people. Never turn down a chance to speak in English and learn from other people about their language-learning techniques.
- Don't overspend. Spending money is not the same as learning.
- Prepare for communication. Preparing for presentations, meetings, phone calls, writing, even social events, will help you communicate more successfully.
- Practise writing. E-mail, chat room, discussion group, …
- Enjoy your learning. The more successfully and confidently you communicate, the more professional and personal pleasure and fulfilment you will derive from the diverse range of contacts we can all build across the world.

Final words about language learning

You don't learn by talking, you learn by listening.
Michael Lewis, English language teacher, author and publisher

Plan → Practise → Review
Gail Ellis and Barbara Sinclair, in *Learning to Learn English*.

Writing task

You are mentoring a young manager virtually. Write a letter or e-mail containing your best advice about how to manage the new team (s)he has just taken over.

F Tips for representing a team

TIPS for delivering good presentations

In Switzerland, there is a political party called the Anti PowerPoint Party which calculates that Europe wastes €110 bn per year from people sitting through dull presentations. Try to reduce the waste by embracing these principles:
- Learn your introduction by heart.
- First say what you're going to say, then say it, then say what you've said.
- Grab the audience's attention in the first three minutes.
- Signal the structure at the beginning and regularly through your talk.
- Give strong stress to key words.
- Be clear about your main message.
- Vary the speed at which you speak. Slow down to emphasise key points.
- Don't let questioners take over the show.
- Be yourself.

TIPS for making presentations across cultures

In some cultures, ...
- audiences prefer just to listen rather than to participate.
- you are expected to be extremely punctual.
- you are expected to spend a lot of time preparing your slides.
- going off the point can be seen as unprofessional.
- there are strict codes about what you should wear.
- there are clear protocols regarding introductions and thanks.
- there may be a negative reaction if seniority is not respected

TIPS for providing feedback on a presentation

You should cover ...
- overall effectiveness
- clarity of message
- organisation: opening – body – close
- level of interest of the content
- use of voice
- visuals
- audience management
- question handling

But first ask the presenter what aspect of the performance (s)he would like to receive feedback on.

TIPS for storytelling

Storytelling can be an effective way to get across the messages that you want to communicate as a leader. You can tell anecdotes, long or short, about yourself or about others, to tell people about your own experience or values, about a learning experience, or to illustrate persistence in the face of adversity.
Here's a short but powerful story:

President John Kennedy once visited NASA (the US National Aeronautics and Space Administration). He came across a cleaner and asked him what his job was. The cleaner replied: 'My job is to help to put a man on the Moon.'

It is not clear whether this story is actually true or not, but what it does illustrate is the cleaner's complete commitment to the aims of NASA, its collective mission and strategy. Do you have any similar stories to tell?

TIPS for managing stress

Too much stress can have an impact on employee attendance (leading to more absence), engagement and retention. Managers need to learn how to deal with stress in themselves and others, and how to handle difficult situations like staff redundancies. British managers have to carry out risk assessments on work-related stress.

Business word combinations

Verb (A–E) + noun
Match each verb from the box with the set of nouns (a–j) it combines best with.

achieve	adopt	boost	bring about	carry out
deal with	develop	enjoy	establish	extend

a .... a customer / an emergency / a (difficult) question / a problem
b .... confidence / morale / productivity / sales
c .... a decision / duties / a plan / a survey
d .... a competence / a partnership with / a process / a team
e .... contact with / a precedent / (good) relations with / a timetable for
f .... a plan / a policy / a proposal / a suggestion
g .... change / an improvement / an increase / a satisfactory outcome
h .... a deadline / a warm welcome to
i .... an aim / a breakthrough / progress / little
j .... (good) relations with / a (good) reputation / success / the support of

Verb (F–J) + noun
Match each verb from the box with the set of nouns (a–j) it combines best with.

face	fail	fix	focus on	gain	guarantee
handle	hold	implement	increase		

a .... a decision / a directive / a plan / a strategy
b .... a deadline / a meeting / a price / a target
c .... experience of / a good reputation / recognition / an advantage
d .... an interview / a meeting / the line / talks with
e .... the details / the essentials / the main issue(s) / the main problem
f .... market share / productivity / sales / client satisfaction
g .... to meet a deadline / to reach a target / a test / an examination
h .... a level of service / quality / satisfaction / success
i .... a challenge / competition from / a delay / difficulties
j .... a problem / a sensitive issue / a difficult situation / a complaint

Verb (K–O) + noun
Match each verb from the box with the set of nouns (a–j) it combines best with.

launch	lead	liaise with	maintain	make
manage	meet	monitor	obtain	offer

a .... an appointment / changes / a complaint / a decision
b .... communication with / an image / pressure on / quality
c .... a commitment / a deadline / customers' expectations / a target
d .... a colleague / an opposite number / a counterpart / head office
e .... assistance / compensation / help / a discount
f .... a campaign / a new initiative / a product / an investigation
g .... approval for / a benefit / permission for/to / support
h .... people / results / time / yourself
i .... performance / progress / a situation / a system
j .... a discussion / a project / a team / a meeting

Verb (P–R) + noun Match each verb from the box with the set of nouns (a–j) it combines best with.

predict	provide	put forward	raise	reach
react to	reduce	resolve	respect	run

a .... conflict / a dispute / a problem / an issue

b .... an agreement / a compromise / a decision / a target

c .... a demand for / a request for / the news that / a situation

d .... failure / success / a result / an outcome

e .... (the level of) awareness of / a question / expectations / prices

f .... someone's opinion / someone's point of view / a deadline / a decision

g .... costs / overheads / the rate of absenteeism / the size of the workforce

h .... a plan / a proposal / a solution / yourself

i .... an estimate / feedback on / a guarantee / help with / support

j .... a company / an organisation / a risk / a scheme

Verb (S–Z) + noun Match each verb from the box with the set of nouns (a–j) it combines best with.

set	set up	sign	submit	support	take
take part in	take up	undertake	weigh up		

a .... a committee / a company / a department / a programme

b .... action against / a break / an initiative / steps to

c .... the advantages and disadvantages / the alternatives / the arguments / the options

d .... a date for delivery / a deadline / standards / a target

e .... an agreement / a contract / a deal / a form

f .... an assignment / research into / a survey / a task

g .... an estimate / a proposal / a report / a request

h .... a discussion / a meeting / a seminar / a workshop

i .... a policy / a proposal / a recommendation / a conference motion

j .... a challenge / an offer / a position / a post

Can you think of more combinations for the verbs on these two pages?

Learning to use these verb + noun combinations will make your professional English more powerful and effective.

Activity file

Unit 1, Section B, Exercise 7

Student A

Role: You are the leader of a marketing project team.

Problem: Andres, one of the programmers in your project team, is not spending enough time on your project. He is finding it difficult because of pressure from his line manager.

Action: You are going to call Andres's manager. Explain that you would like Andres to spend one day a week on your project. Try to get the manager's agreement to this.

Spend a few minutes preparing before you call. Think about the Four Ps and the stages in the communication process.

Unit 2, Section B, Exercise 10

Your name: ....

Your job: ....

Your company: ....

Your location: ....

Your nationality: ....

The main challenges in your job: ....

Your family: ....

Your main interests outside work: ....

Unit 5, Section C, Exercise 7

Student C

Observer

You are going to observe the five-minute dialogue between Student A and Student B, then give Student A feedback. Student A is going to try and persuade Student B to buy the product or service (s)he has identified. Pay attention to how much talking Student A and Student B do. Successful influencing and selling both depend on listening, but you may well find that Student A does more talking than listening and makes more statements than asking questions. Base on your feedback on this and on how convinced Student B seems to have been by Student A's approach.

Unit 7, Section B, Exercise 9

Observer

You should establish your own criteria for giving feedback. However, you might like to think about these factors:

- **Process**
  Were procedures clearly established and followed? Was time managed well?
- **Purpose**
  Were there clear and positive outcomes? Why? / Why not?
- **People**
  Were contributions well-managed? balanced? What can you say to help people develop?

Unit 1, Section D, Exercise 2

Other layers of the culture onion could be:
- sector
- company
- professional/functional
- gender
- age
- religion
- political affiliation
- region
- class
- ethnic group
- special interest

Unit 3, Section C, Exercise 9

	quality in order of importance To be:	% importance	% of managers seen as competent
1	approachable	83	50
2	a good communicator	82	28
3	supportive	81	38
4	a good leader	80	31
5	respectful of each individual	76	36

Unit 4, Section B, Exercise 7

Group A
You are a group of consultants commissioned by a company to make proposals about how to improve the effectiveness of its meetings. Come up with a list of ideas for improvement. Your list should include one or more of the ideas below. When you have finalised your list, meet with the other group and agree on a joint list. You want as many of your suggestions as possible to be in the final list.
- Think about the purpose. If you don't really have anything to discuss at the weekly meeting, don't hold it that week.
- Abolish chairs. Have everyone stand at the meeting.
- Encourage punctuality. Lock the door five minutes after the meeting has started so latecomers cannot enter.

Unit 7, Section C, Exercise 7

Role C
Read the role cards for Student A on page 97 and for Student B on page 95. You are going to observe their meeting. Think in advance about how you think such an interview should be managed and what outcome both people should be trying to achieve. Listen to the kind of language they both use and, in your feedback afterwards, tell them what you think about both the outcome and about how helpful their language was in achieving it.

Unit 7, Section D, Case study

Role B: President of the clothing division
You are keen to create a successful business operation which will lead to significantly improved sales and reduced costs. However, each of the local companies is concerned that the high level of commitment of their employees is bound to decline. You have brought in the consultant in order to get the three subsidiaries to agree to the concept of a streamlined operation. You can be a bit impatient and suspicious of too much talk about corporate culture.

Communication styles

formal ←→ informal
indirect ←→ direct
emotional ←→ neutral
time-focused ←→ time-flexible
distanced ←→ personal
proactive ←→ reactive
expansive ←→ concise
content-oriented ←→ relation-oriented
organic ←→ systematic
complex ←→ simple
participative ←→ silent
facilitating ←→ assertive

These notes are intended as reference for terms which you are not sure about. Don't try to read them all, just the ones that you need.

- More **formal** communicators prefer to use more traditionally 'correct' language and may well also dress in a more conservative way. More **informal** communicators prefer a more relaxed style, both in terms of the kind of language used and possibly also in terms of dress, posture, etc.
- More **indirect** communicators tend to use conditionals (*I would think so*), modals (*Could you ...?* rather than *Can you ...?*) and words like *possibly*, *perhaps* and *maybe* in order to reduce the force and impact of what they are saying. More **direct** communicators tend to use straight simple statements or closed questions and to avoid spending time on matters not directly related to the main subject of the communication.
- More **emotional** communicators like to show their feelings about what they are communicating. More **neutral** communicators prefer not to show their feelings about what they are communicating.
- More **time-focused** communicators prefer to define in advance how much time should be given to a specific communication event. More **time-flexible** communicators are happy not to define in advance how long a given communication event should last.
- More **distanced** communicators prefer to discuss work-related or neutral subjects, especially with relative strangers. More **personal** communicators like to talk about non-professional subjects with new contacts, often including their own thoughts and feelings, as a way of getting to know them.
- More **proactive** communicators tend to take the initiative in communication. More **reactive** communicators tend to wait for someone else to take the initiative in communication.
- More **expansive** communicators prefer to say more rather than less. They enjoy words for their own sake. More **concise** communicators prefer to say less rather than more. They enjoy being economical with words.
- More **content-oriented** communicators prefer to focus on the task dimension in communication. More **relation-oriented** communicators prefer to focus on the people dimension in communication.
- More **organic** communicators prefer communication to be unplanned and spontaneous. More **systematic** communicators prefer to have a clear structure to any communication.
- More **complex** communicators prefer to convey information of a specialised nature in an efficient manner without paraphrase or explanation. More **simple** communicators try to adapt the density of content, style and language of the communication to the likely level of understanding of the listener.
- More **participative** listeners like to send positive and supportive signals in terms of facial expression, body language and verbal language to the person who is talking. More **silent** listeners tend not to send signals of any kind to the person who is speaking.
- More **facilitating** communicators like to encourage other people to communicate. More **assertive** communicators like to play a dominant role in communication.

Unit 7, Section D, Case study

> **Role D: management representative from the French ski manufacturer**
> You work for a company which was founded and run by enthusiastic specialists. Now you are part of a much bigger organisation and you are worried that your part of the company is going to lose its identity and that the high current level of engagement of the employees is bound to decline.
> You plan to tell the other people at the meeting in very direct terms that you and your colleagues are extremely concerned about the future and also very demotivated.

Unit 5, Section B, Exercise 9a

> **Team A**
> **Buyers**
> You work for Yorkwear as purchasing managers for Europe.
>
> *Background*
> Yorkwear is a major British fashion retail chain, based in York. You have established contacts with Acme Clothing, a Swiss-based clothing designer and manufacturer. You were very impressed with their range of exclusive ties in their new 'Supply Chain' collection at last month's fair in Zurich. You have been quoted a unit price of €5, including the cost of shipping and insurance, and you want to place an order for 100,000 ties from the collection.
>
> *Situation*
> It is now the end of October, and you need the ties quickly, in order to launch the collection on your UK shelves in time for Christmas. The third week in November is ideal for this kind of launch. You know that your target customer loves bright colours and modern designs, and they expect to be able to choose from a wide range of pattern types.
>
> *Task*
> Your objective is to conclude a satisfactory deal for the specified quantity of 100,000. Note that your market is very competitive, so beware of making too many concessions which will add to your costs.
> Use the following scoring system as a guide to your priorities and aim to collect as many points as possible. Take some time to plan objectives, negotiating limits and strategy accordingly.
>
> | Delivery | Points/Priorities |
> |---|---|
> | before Nov. 29 | 7 |
> | Nov. 30–Dec. 6 | 3 |
> | Dec. 7–12 | 2 |
> | **Number of patterns** | |
> | 9–10 | 5 |
> | 6–8 | 3 |
> | 3–5 | 2 |
> | **Number of colours** | |
> | 15–20 | 6 |
> | 11–14 | 5 |
> | 5–10 | 2 |
> | **Payment** | |
> | 60 days | 3 |
> | 30 days | 2 |
> | at sight | 1 |
> | **Discount** | |
> | Above 30% | 7 |
> | 15%–25% | 5 |
> | 10% | 3 |
> | less than 8% | 2 |

Team B
Sellers
You work for Acme Clothing as sales managers for Northern Europe.

Background
Acme Clothing is a well-known Swiss clothing designer and manufacturer based in Zurich. You operate in a highly competitive market and have recently been losing market share to Stevovic, a Czech-based company. Therefore, you are very pleased to have made a new contact with Yorkwear, a major British clothing retail chain, which seems very interested in placing a major order for 100,000 ties from your exclusive 'Supply Chain' range at a unit price of €5.

Situation
Acme is facing some cashflow problems at the moment. It is the end of October, and you desperately need to get money into the organisation. You realise that Yorkwear will require the ties urgently in order to launch on the Christmas market. However, you have a number of orders with existing customers – with which you are behind schedule – meaning you would prefer not to guarantee delivery of any consignment before 6 December.
You expect Yorkwear to ask for ties designed in a wide variety of colours and patterns. You can meet this demand, but there are cost implications, as you will need to employ more manufacturing staff. Any discounts would have to take account of this.

Task
Your objective is to conclude a satisfactory deal for the specified quantity of 100,000. Use the following scoring system as a guide to your priorities and aim to collect as many points as possible. Take some time to plan objectives, negotiating limits and strategy accordingly.

Delivery	Points/Priorities
before Nov. 24	1
Nov. 25–Dec. 5	2
Dec. 6–10	4

Number of patterns	
More than 12	1
6–8	4
4–5	5

Number of colours	
more than 18	1
10–13	5
fewer than 7	9

Payment	
60 days	2
30 days	4
at sight	6

Discount	
over 25%	1
10%–15%	3
less than 10%	6

Unit 5, Section C, Exercise 7

Student A
Seller
You are going to spend five minutes trying to sell a product or service to Student B. Student B will tell you what the product is. Student C will observe and give you feedback when you finish.

Unit 7, Section C, Exercise 7

Role B

You have worked for Student A, your manager, in the same job for a number of years and have generally had an acceptable record of performance. You have never felt very inspired by your job, but you are happy to have a regular income and job security. Recently, however, your health has been poor, due to some domestic problems, which have sometimes left you feeling depressed. You have also been finding it more difficult to concentrate and feel motivated at work.

You have not told Student A about this. (S)he is clearly concerned about your performance and has now asked you to attend a meeting. Think about what you expect from your manager and from the organisation before you role-play the meeting.

Unit 4, Section B, Exercise 7

Group B

You are a group of consultants commissioned by a company to make proposals about how to improve the effectiveness of its meetings. Come up with a list of ideas for improvement. Your list should include one or more of the ideas below. When you have finalised your list, meet with the other group and agree on a joint list. You want as many of your suggestions as possible to be in the final list.

- Encourage punctuality. Make people who are more than five minutes late pay a sum of money which will go to charity.
- Make meetings optional. Allow people to decide for themselves whether they should attend or not.
- Decide what's useful. Walk out if you don't think the meeting is useful to you. (If you make it a house rule, people won't think you're rude.)

Unit 7, Section B, Exercise 9

Participants

- Each of you should choose a work-related leadership issue or challenge which you can present to the meeting. Your objective is to get useful ideas from your colleagues on how to deal with it. Choose a problem which is not too technical so that everyone will be able to understand and advise on it.
- In turn, lead the meeting for 15 minutes.
- When it is your turn:
  - present your item (*2–3 minutes*)
  - answer questions to clarify the details (*1–2 minutes*)
  - guide the discussion without stating your own opinions or actions (*8–10 minutes*)
  - when time is up, summarise the main recommendations you have received (*1–2 minutes*).
  - hand over to the next chair.

Unit 1, Section B, Exercise 7

Student B

Role: You are the manager of an IT department.

Problem: You are concerned about one of your programmers, Andres, because he is not productive enough.

Action: You are about to receive a call from the leader of a marketing project team about Andres. You know a little about this project that Andres and this manager are involved in.

Spend a few minutes preparing before you take the call. Think about the Four Ps and the stages in the communication process.

Unit 7, Section D, Case study

> **Role C: management representative from Portland Sports**
> You work for a company which was founded and run by enthusiastic specialists. Now you are part of a much bigger organisation and you are worried that your part of the company is going to lose its identity and that the high current level of engagement of the employees is bound to decline.
> You hope that the two-day meeting will give you an opportunity to express your concerns. You think that the meeting could be an opportunity to ensure some protection for your local identity, but you also feel quite threatened.

Unit 1, Section B, Exercise 7

> **Student C**
> You will observe Students A and B during the exercise, so you should read both their role cards (see pages 90 and 95). Your job is to give them feedback on their communication performance. How successful do you think their communication was? Give feedback using the checklists provided by Jeremy Comfort:
> 1 Give them your overall evaluation of their performance. Was the communication successful? What did they do well? What could they improve?
> 2 Did they respect the three Ps? ('People roles' do not need to be defined here.)
> 3 Did they go through all the stages in the communication process? Did they need to? Would it have helped if they had spent less or more time on one of the stages?
>   1 Preparation
>   2 Opening
>   3 Relationship building
>   4 Structuring
>   5 Discussing and negotiating
>   6 Deciding
>   7 Concluding and summarising
>   8 Closing
>   9 Celebrating

Unit 5, Section C, Exercise 7

> **Student B**
> **Buyer**
> Student A is going to spend five minutes trying to sell you a product or service. Student C will observe and give feedback to Student A when you have finished. You can give feedback to Student A as well after Student C. Choose one from this list of products and services and tell Student A what you have chosen:
> ● a new car
> ● a Mediterranean cruise
> ● solar panels for your home
> ● an intensive language training course in the UK

Unit 7, Section D, Case study

> **Role E: management representative from the Canadian golf-equipment manufacturer**
> You work for a company which was founded and run by enthusiastic specialists. Now you are part of a much bigger organisation and you are worried that your part of the company is going to lose its identity and that the high current level of engagement of the employees is bound to decline.
> You are very sceptical about the value of this meeting and you doubt that anything will be achieved by it. You will point out to the others when you think that time is being wasted and when the important issues are not being dealt with.

Unit 7, Section C, Exercise 7

Role A

You are Student B's manager. Student B has been working in the same job in your department for a number of years and has generally had an acceptable but average record of performance. More recently, Student B's performance has started to become erratic. (S)he is more often late to work or absent, forgets details, and fails to deliver work on time. You have discussed these issues with Student B in the past and even tried some coaching, but you have not seen any real change.

You have now invited Student B to a formal interview, where you plan to confront the issue of underperformance. Role-play the interview with Student B.

Unit 7, Section D, Case study

Role A: consultant

You are the consultant. Your job is to facilitate a two-day meeting for about 20 people, which will achieve the objectives of your client (the President of the clothing division). You know that the representatives of the three subsidiaries have little knowledge of each other, and are concerned that their brands and identities are under threat. Discuss with your colleagues an agenda for the two-day meeting and an action plan for achieving a common culture. Your first loyalty is, of course, to your client.

Audio script

UNIT 1

Track 1

Interviewer: Hélène, you've been in management for quite a few years. Could you start by telling us what a manager is?

Hélène: That's a good question. It's easy to make life very complicated when talking about this. For me, a manager is someone who gets results through other people. Another way to put it could be: the job of a manager is to lead a team to achieve planned objectives.

Interviewer: That makes managing sound very simple in theory. Why can it be so difficult in practice?

Hélène: I think one problem is that people become managers because they are good at their jobs – because they have some kind of special expertise. So then they get promoted to be in charge of a group of other people, but that means they suddenly need a completely new set of skills – soft skills, people skills, communication skills ... which they may not have.

Interviewer: So are managers born or can they be made? Can we train people to be managers?

Hélène: Oh, I'm sure that we can teach people this – provided they want to learn. Although I think it's important for people to be able to make the choice between becoming a manager or not. Not everyone enjoys doing it or wants to do it, so we shouldn't criticise people who decide that management is not for them – we should respect that decision.

Track 2

Interviewer: How did you feel when you first moved into a management position?

Hélène: I was very nervous – quite anxious about it. All the people in the team were older than me and had all been in the company much longer than me. They all had their own way of doing things.

Interviewer: And what did you find most difficult?

Hélène: Making time for other people when I had my own job to do. But I learned MBWA.

Interviewer: Which is?

Hélène: Management By Walking Around. You know, in France we shake hands with everyone every morning, and so I would leave time to go round to say *bonjour* to everyone in my team. They knew that if there was anything they wanted to talk about, they could raise it then. I have a much bigger team now, but I still do it – sometimes it can take a couple of hours before I get to my office, but it is worth it!

Interviewer: And did you learn anything else?

Hélène: I learned from my mistakes! Or rather, I tried to think about what I was doing and to reflect. And if I or anyone else made a mistake, I tried to encourage us all to ... to help each other, to learn from the experience, rather than blaming anybody. At least until you made the same mistake for the third time, then you need to take a different kind of action!

Track 3

Interviewer: Jeremy, you've thought a lot about business communication. What do you think we need to understand about communication at work?

Jeremy: I certainly believe that people should spend more time thinking about communication. Everyone agrees that the key to getting people more involved and getting better results from them is good communication, but a lot of managers don't think about communication very much.

Interviewer: Can we learn to be better communicators? What do we need to understand?

Jeremy: Yes, I think we can all learn to communicate better. Part of it is understanding more about how to ensure good communication. I like to talk about the four Ps. With these, your business communication can get progressively better.

Interviewer: What are they?

Jeremy: The first P is Preparation. A lot of people feel that they waste a lot of time in meetings, for example. This can be a problem when they're not thinking in advance about how best to manage the time available. If someone can circulate a clearly written agenda and relevant documentation in advance, tell people what they need to get ready, tell them when the meeting should start and finish, how much time will be devoted to each point and so on, things are likely to go much better than if they aren't done.

Interviewer: OK, and the next one?

Jeremy: My second P is Purpose. Everyone should be absolutely clear *why* they're doing what they're doing. Why are we having this meeting? What exactly are we trying to achieve in this negotiation? What's the purpose of this presentation? Quite often people aren't at all clear about what outcomes they're supposed to be working towards.

Interviewer: And P number 3?

Jeremy: This is Process, and I think this is the aspect of communication which can be most neglected. You see this a lot in international meetings, when people don't know each other very well. Some people expect to start on time, others don't. Some expect a strong lead from the chair, others think the chair should keep a low profile. Some think it's OK to answer phone calls during the meeting, others think that's very rude. If people don't agree on processes in these situations, there's the risk of a lot of misunderstanding, confusion, frustration, even anger.

Interviewer: And the last P?

Jeremy: Last but not least is People. People need to be clear about what they are supposed to do. It's very important that there's agreement in these different communication situations about who does what. If people's roles aren't clarified at the outset, there's a further risk of problems arising, either straightaway or later on. We all need to be clear about not only where we want to go, but also how we're going to get there and what contribution each of us is expected to make to achieve the common goal.

Track 4

Interviewer: So we should use the Four Ps as a checklist in the different communication situations at work.

Jeremy: That's right.

Interviewer: Do you have any other ideas to help people communicate better at work?

Jeremy: I think it can help if people see what different communication situations have in common – the fact that there's a common process in the different things we do: meeting, phoning, writing – even socialising.

Interviewer: Can you describe it?

Jeremy: Sure. First of all, preparation is important – for a presentation, a negotiation, a phone call. You have to organise in advance, and the more important it is, the more you prepare. Then, when you actually start the meeting or whatever it is, there's an opening. It could be a very brief ice-breaker or greeting or personal introduction, but that's important too.

Then there's a relationship-building stage – it could be just an exchange of remarks about the weather on the phone with someone you know well, or it could be a critical phase lasting days or weeks if you're doing business in, say, the Middle East. Then there's a structuring phase in which you outline or agree how you're going to proceed.

And then there's the main meat of the event – discussing and negotiating – to do the main business. This leads us to the deciding phase, followed by the very important need for concluding and summarising – summarising what has been agreed, so that all parties are clear about the outcome. Then closing the event. And then sometimes – at least, if it was a big event – celebrating, although maybe we don't want to do that after an e-mail or a phone call!

I think if people can use this as a checklist for managing communication, it can help them improve the process and also understand better what to do when things go wrong.

UNIT 2

Track 5

Interviewer: Anindita, can you tell us how you go about building a new team?

Anindita Gupta: I think building a team is both simple and complex. In some ways it's easy, and in other ways it's very hard work. Of course, you need to be clear about goals and roles and so on. But I think there are two important aspects which you can't neglect. The first is getting to know people in the team. Good relationships and mutual respect help to make strong teams. When I'm starting to work with a new project team, I always try and organise an away-day or some other opportunity for us all to get to know each other – not necessarily talking about work at all, but getting to know about people's backgrounds, finding things we have in common – that sort of thing.

The second is getting people to understand that strong teams really benefit from having different kinds of people in them. When we can accept that other team members are different from us – in the way they work and the way they see the world – I think that we start to understand how that diversity can benefit us all.

Interviewer: And how do you get people to see this? How do you achieve it?

Anindita Gupta: I think some of the standard team development tools which are available like the Myers Briggs Type Indicator and also the Margerison-McCann Team Management Profile are very good for this, and I use them a lot.

Interviewer: Could you tell us a bit more about one of them?

Anindita Gupta: Well, they're both psychometric questionnaires. The Team Management Profile helps you and your colleagues by looking at four aspects of the way you like to work.

Firstly, in terms of the way we like to relate to other people – relationships: it finds out how far you're an introvert or an extrovert. Nobody is completely introvert or completely extrovert, of course, but most of us do tend to be more on one side than the other – and some of us are quite in the middle.

Secondly, in terms of how we gather and use information: some of us do this in a more practical way and some of us in a more creative way.

Thirdly, in terms of the way we make decisions: some of us tend to take decisions more analytically – with our heads – and some of us take decisions more according to our beliefs or feelings – with our hearts.

And finally, it looks at how we organise ourselves and others at work. Some of us do this in a more structured way, and some of us do it in a more flexible way. By combining an understanding of how people prefer to approach work with the key success factors that form the basis of successful teamwork, the Profile really helps team development.

Interviewer: And why do you think knowing this about yourself and others in the team is helpful?

Anindita Gupta: I think because it helps you to be tolerant of difference. For example, I know that I'm quite creative, a 'big picture' person, so I'm good at coming up with lots of ideas. But I also know that I'm not so good at following through on these ideas and getting them translated into action. So I work very well with a colleague who's much more structured and organised than I am, much more of a 'details' person, so that I produce the ideas and he makes sure they get implemented. That's putting it very simply, but the tool has helped us to appreciate each other rather than struggle, because we had different ways of seeing the world.

Track 6

Interviewer: Birgit, you're German and you've worked all your professional life for a company in Düsseldorf, is that right?

Birgit Schmidt: Well, apart from two years in another company when I left school, that's right.

Interviewer: So please, could you tell us about how you and your colleagues relate to each other in the workplace?

Birgit Schmidt: Well, the way we relate to each other is quite formal here. I still address my older colleagues as *Frau* or *Herr* – Mr or Mrs. We tend to use the polite form of *you* in German with each other – *Sie* rather than *du*. And we tend to make a clear distinction between work and life outside work. So I don't know much about the private lives of my colleagues at work, and they don't know much about mine.

Interviewer: And do you like working like this? Some people may find this different from what they're used to, maybe strange.

Birgit Schmidt: I suppose I'm used to it, but I think we base our work relationships on respect. This is very important. I try to do a good job in order to earn the respect of my colleagues. And I like this.

Interviewer: And are things the same as they used to be?

Birgit Schmidt: No, I think things are changing. I've been in the company for 25 years and I'm in my 50s. Younger people are less formal with each other. They don't make such a clear distinction between work and outside work as my generation does.

Interviewer: And how do you feel about this?

Birgit Schmidt: Sometimes I feel a bit uncomfortable when I hear people at work being more familiar than I'm used to. But the younger engineers are generally careful to speak to older people like me in a different way than they talk to each other. In a way, I quite like the way things are changing – it makes people less stiff and more relaxed, I think.

Track 7

Interviewer: But you also have an international dimension to your job, don't you? Can you tell us something about that?

Birgit Schmidt: Yes, I'm a member of our company's European Works Council.

Interviewer: Which is ...?

Birgit Schmidt: It's a committee of employee representatives from the different European countries where our company is present. About 25 of us from the different countries meet once a year to discuss things with management. Some of us have to work through interpreters, but I've still got to know some people from France, Spain, Italy, the UK and Poland quite well. And some of us meet more than once a year.

Interviewer: Do you enjoy it?

Birgit Schmidt: Very much. Although the communication can be challenging sometimes.

Interviewer: And is communication very formal in this situation, too?

Birgit Schmidt: It's very formal in the big meetings, but that's partly because there are a lot of people and we work through interpreters. But outside the meeting room, it's very different, because we're usually there for two days or more and eat together in the hotel and socialise and so on.

Interviewer: Mm. And are the relationships formal here as well?

Birgit Schmidt: Um, it depends to some extent on where people come from, and also some people are quite shy about speaking English or another foreign language. But some of the other members are very informal and very warm, and we've got to know them pretty well over the last few years.

Interviewer: Can you tell us how some of them are different?

Birgit Schmidt: I think that the people from Italy and Spain, for example, have a different way of dealing with people. They seemed much less formal than I was used to when I first met them; and I think it's also more important for some of them to get to know the people they're working with – personally, as people. So we spend more time socialising with them and catching up with each other. I think a lot of Germans tend to be quite focused on the task when we meet, but some of our colleagues need to know who they're dealing with before they get down to business.

Interviewer: Mm. And how do you deal with this?

Birgit Schmidt: I think we've come to accept and understand it. And we now do relationship-building exercises from time to time to help new people become full members of the group. So I think we see the importance of this.

UNIT 3

Track 8

Interviewer: Please, would you tell us what you do?

Alfredo: Yes, I am the Production Manager in a chemicals factory about 60 kilometres from Mexico City. It's a German multinational company. I've been doing this job about four years.

Interviewer: How many people work in the factory? How many people are you responsible for?

Alfredo: There are 350 people in the factory and about 500 on the site altogether. I report to the Production Director, but I have the day-to-day responsibility for all the process workers.

Interviewer: We want to ask you about leadership in the business. Is there a strong sense of direction in your part of the organisation? Do you feel that people know where they're going?

Alfredo: I'd say that, from the top to the bottom, there's a strong sense of direction. We can start with the vision and values of the organisation, which come from the company in Germany and which you can see everywhere in the factory and in the offices, on the intranet and in the company's bulletins and newsletters. We're also given very clear production and cost targets for the year and we work to these. And we have to do a lot of reporting to the head office – weekly, monthly, quarterly – to show how we're doing.

Interviewer: And so how do *you* provide direction?

Alfredo: The communication in our company is generally top-down and, in Mexico, many managers like me are quite directive. You tell people what to do, and they do it. Our business is organised to maximise shareholder value, so targets can be challenging, and our job is to deliver on those targets. Information and goals both come down through the organisation from the boardroom to the shop floor.

Track 9

Interviewer: Can you tell us what you do?

Eva: Yes, I'm the secretary and administrator for the management team of a big international construction project in Stockholm. I manage the liaison between the management team and the zones where the construction is going on and also with the contractors – Swedish ones and others from Germany and Denmark.

Interviewer: And how many people are involved in the project altogether?

Eva: Um, it's about 500.

Interviewer: Where does direction come from in your organisation?

Eva: Well, we have a very clear goal, which is to complete a major public construction project right in the centre of Stockholm in the next five years, so a lot of the direction comes from this and from the project plan. But the regular decision-making goes on in the management committee. That's a group of 15 people, including the project leader, the zone engineers, the environment, communication, purchasing and finance officers, and so on.

Interviewer: Does the project leader make all the decisions?

Eva: Not at all! We do it the Swedish way, with a lot of discussion before every big decision and with everyone saying what they think before we come to a decision all together. So sometimes it can take quite a time to decide, but once we have, everyone is committed to it because everyone has agreed to it.

Interviewer: Mm. But isn't it still a top-down process, because you're still telling the other people what to do once you've decided?

Eva: Well, not really, because the zone engineers will already have talked to their own people, so they will tell us what the others think and we'll take that into consideration.

Track 10

Interviewer: Alfredo, how do you communicate direction to your people?

Alfredo: I think this is very important for a manager, especially in production. People need to know exactly what they have to do. So I have a daily meeting with my team leaders – every morning at the start of the shift – and we go through what we have to do that day and we also review what happened the day before.

Interviewer: And what happens exactly? Who does the most talking?

Alfredo: Well, basically, I tell them what to do, because I have already talked to the Production Director, so I am relaying what we discussed. But I have two rules for how I try to communicate. The first is that I try to be as clear as possible. If I start using complicated language, some of the supervisors are not going to understand. I learned in English 'K.I.S.S.' – Keep It Short and Simple, or Keep It Simple, Stupid. This is a very good approach, I think.

Interviewer: And the second rule you have?

Alfredo: I always try to give the right context to what I say when I'm talking to my people. Sometimes when I'm listening to managers from the head office, I don't understand what they're saying, because they're talking about things that we don't know anything about. And it's difficult to ask them to explain, because they might think you're just stupid. So when I'm talking to my people, I always try to think: What do they know about this? What don't they know about this? What do they need to know? You have to give a

context and you have to get the level of information right. I think this is a big communication challenge for a lot of managers, in fact for most people, really.

Interviewer: Can you describe your communication style?

Alfredo: That's a difficult question ... mm, I think I'm direct, serious, careful ... er, I try to organise what I want to say. Some of my colleagues aren't so organised when they talk. It drives me crazy.

Track 11

Interviewer: Eva, how do you communicate direction to your people?

Eva: Well, they're not really my people, since I'm not the manager of the project. But I do have to make sure that everyone knows what's going on and what has been decided.

Interviewer: So what do you do? How do you achieve that?

Eva: I talk a lot! A lot of my job is talking and listening. Everyone knows they can phone me if they have any questions about anything, because they know that I talk to Matthias – he's the project leader – every day and that I know what is going on.

Interviewer: So in a way you are communicating *for* him, is that right?

Eva: Yes, I help him by helping other people to get the information they need, so he doesn't have too many people to talk to every day.

Interviewer: What is your own communication style? How would you describe it?

Eva: Um, like I said, I talk a lot on the phone and I walk around the offices a lot, chatting to people, and I try to think: Who needs to know this? And I try not to do too much e-mailing, because everyone has too many e-mails to deal with these days. So I have a quite informal style. As I said, I love to talk. Actually, I like to listen a lot as well, so I ask a *lot* of questions.

Interviewer: Do people like your style?

Eva: I think so. We work very hard as a team. We're all very dedicated to the project's success. I think some of the contractors were surprised at the beginning to see how we talk ... how I talk!

Interviewer: And how did you react to that?

Eva: I tried to be more serious with them. Yes, I tried to adapt and I asked them if they were happy with this way of communicating. I asked them for feedback, and now we have a good way of working together with the contractors as well.

UNIT 4

Track 12

Interviewer: Fernando, can you tell us what you do?

Fernando: Yes, I work for one of the biggest mobile telecoms companies in Mexico. I'm an engineer and started here after my studies. Last year, I was put in charge of a group of engineers involved in network maintenance.

Interviewer: How many people are there in your team?

Fernando: There are nine engineers and one secretary in our group.

Interviewer: We're interested in how people organise the work of the team, so can you tell us why being well organised is important, and then tell us how you do this?

Fernando: I think this is a difficult thing for a young manager to do. But it's a critical part of the manager's job, because people need to be clear about their objectives and how they are going to achieve these objectives.

Interviewer: So what did you do?

Fernando: At first I made mistakes. It seemed like I had two jobs – my own technical work and managing other people's – and I wasn't so good at giving clear instructions. But then I told myself that management is simply getting results from people, so I spent more time on planning and began to delegate more.

Interviewer: How much time do you spend on planning, say, for the coming week?

Fernando: At first, I spent all the weekend! But now we have a debrief meeting on Friday afternoon and a planning meeting on Monday morning and we work very much together. So I don't spend more than a couple of hours on it now, between the two meetings.

Interviewer: Do you communicate the plan for the week to the whole team on Monday morning?

Fernando: Yes, we have a one-hour meeting, and I try to be very clear about what the team has to do and what each person has to do.

Interviewer: And did you delegate some of the technical work you used to do, so that you can spend more time on managing?

Fernando: Yes, I did; although over the year, I've tried to encourage my colleagues to feel that they're being empowered, rather than just having work delegated to them.

Interviewer: What's the difference?

Fernando: Well, what I understand is that when you delegate, you give the task to someone else, but you keep the responsibility for it. When you empower someone, they take on the task and they take responsibility for it as well – they own it.

Interviewer: OK ... And finally, what's your biggest challenge when it comes to organising work?

Fernando: At the moment, I think we're still not working in the best way. I want us to spend more time talking about *how* we work, not just *what* we are doing. For example, we could be running our meetings better than we do.

Track 13

Oleg: Well, that was another waste of time!

Renate: Yes, someone is really going to have to talk to Nick about these meetings.

Oleg: Why can't you do it?

Renate: OK, I'll do it if you and the others back me up.

Oleg: I'm sure everyone will support you. We're all really fed up with it.

Renate: So what shall I say?

Oleg: Where do we start? I think the main problem is that there is usually no agenda, so no one has any information about where to go or what to prepare ... or anything!

Renate: OK, I'll make that point first. And even when there is an agenda, I still have no idea what we are going to be talking about. Just putting 'Finance', for

example, doesn't tell us what exactly we're going to discuss.

Oleg: Right. Sometimes I don't know what the meeting is for and I don't know who's supposed to be there.

Renate: Yes, we don't get any papers in advance. And more than once, we've turned up to find the room hasn't been booked – and you know what a problem it is when you haven't booked.

Oleg: And so we find a room and then Nick always turns up 15 minutes late, as if nothing had happened!

Renate: Yes, I think there's quite a lot to talk about. But do you think it will make any difference?

Oleg: Come on, Renate, you've got to make him understand how frustrated everyone is. You can do it!

UNIT 5

Track 14

Indira: Indira Kapoor.

Ana: Hello, Indira. It's Ana. Do you have some time to talk?

Indira: Of course, Ana. Nice to hear from you. How are you?

Ana: Oh, I'm OK, thanks. But I wanted to talk to you about the new branding project.

Indira: The one we've just launched? Is everything OK?

Ana: Well, that's what I want to talk to you about. You know we work hard to reach our targets here, and I think we're doing a good job.

Indira: Yes, the German figures are great.

Ana: Of course, it's demanding, and I'm out of the office quite a lot. But now I've just seen the timetable for the branding project. It's not just that the targets are ambitious – it's going to take up a lot of time, too, and I just don't see how I can fit it all in.

Indira: OK, Ana, I understand the point you're making, but you have to talk to Marie in Paris. You report to her on this.

Ana: Yes, I know, and I've tried. I ... I don't want to seem to be going over her head, but she's really difficult to get hold of and even more difficult to pin down.

Indira: I know what you mean.

Ana: I'm worried about getting into a situation where I have three jobs to do and I'm not doing any of them properly. I have a problem with the matrix organisation here. You see, I now report to three different people on three different projects, and there doesn't seem to be very much communication between them. And it's all creating stress for me – and for my colleagues here too. It's really a problem of work–life balance.

Indira: OK, so those are the problems. What are the solutions?

Ana: I knew you'd say that. You always do. Well, I think the best approach might be ...

Track 15

Marie: Allô?

Ana: Hello, is that Marie?

Marie: Yes. Is that Ana?

Ana: Yes, hello Marie.

Marie: Hello Ana, nice to hear from you. How's the family?

Ana: Oh, they're all fine, thanks. And yours?

Marie: Yes, they're all fine, thanks. What I can do for you? I'm sorry I've been so difficult to reach recently.

Ana: That's OK. I wanted to talk about the branding project.

Marie: OK. You know, we really appreciate the job you're doing. You're like a mentor to some of those younger managers.

Ana: It's nice of you to say so. I want to help, but I'm concerned about the other parts of my job – our sales drive in Germany and the other projects I'm busy with.

Marie: How do you want to proceed?

Ana: I'd like us to agree on my objectives for this project, on my role and on my time allocation – especially in relation to the travel and the meetings.

Marie: Doesn't the timetable I sent out cover this?

Ana: Some of it, yes; but no one has talked to me about what's really possible in all this. I'm already quite stretched, and this is going to need a lot of extra time.

Marie: OK, my proposal is, first of all, that you act as the deputy leader of the project, so that you can take responsibility for everything in my absence. That would give the others a clear sense that a leader is always available.

Ana: Does that mean that you want me to be at all the meetings? You're planning a progress meeting every two months, right?

Marie: Yes, in different countries. But I also see your main objective as being the transfer of your expertise. I want you to teach the six younger managers in Europe what you know.

Ana: And how much time will all this take?

Marie: The meetings will be a day, plus travel. I'll look after the sales targets, but for the mentoring, I had in mind something like an hour a month with each of them.

Ana: Six hours a month and a one-day meeting every two months … it's a lot.

Marie: It's a really important project, Ana. We have to have a strong commitment to innovation and to professional development to achieve that.

Ana: I know, but I have a strong commitment to sales in Germany as well! I like doing this kind of mentoring, but I don't think the project needs a deputy and I don't think I need to go to every meeting. I suggest that I attend the meetings virtually, by conference call, and just sit in on the parts which are relevant to me, not the whole day.

Marie: I could agree to that if you could be there for the first kick-off meeting.

Ana: OK, so to summarise, I'll sit in on all meetings by conference call, apart from the initial one, then you'll run the project on your own and the progress meetings as well. OK?

Marie: Yes, I'm happy with that.

Ana: OK, great. Speak to you soon. Bye!

Marie: Yes, Goodbye!

UNIT 6

Track 16

Tanja: OK, Alex, what would you like to talk about today?

Alex: I'd like to talk about the benefits report I have to write for Vladimir.

Tanja: OK, so what's the issue?

Alex: I should have given it to Vladimir a week ago.

Tanja: And what outcome do you want to get from this session?

Alex: I need a plan to get it done as soon as possible.

Tanja: Mm-hm. Um, what's the current situation?

Alex: We're very busy in the office here. There are always interruptions. I have to get data from the other countries, but people don't send it.

Tanja: How long will the report be?

Alex: Oh, er, somewhere around 30 pages. I'm not sure …

Tanja: Alex, think about it. How long is the report?

Alex: It should be about 25 pages.

Tanja: Mm-hm. How much have you done so far?

Alex: Two pages.

Tanja: What do you need to get the job done?

Alex: More time! And no interruptions.

Tanja: How much time do you need to finish it?

Alex: Mm, maybe a week.

Tanja: Imagine that you didn't have any interruptions at all. How much time would it take then?

Alex: It's hard to say. It takes me a long time to write in English.

Tanja: No interruptions. How long?

Alex: Maybe two days.

Tanja: Maybe?

Alex: OK, two days. If I could get the data.

Tanja: And how long will that take?

Alex: Forever. Some people never answer my e-mails.

Tanja: So what do you need to do to get the data?

Alex: I don't know. Maybe Vladimir could tell them. Or you.

Tanja: Can I solve this for you?

Alex: No.

Tanja: Or Vladimir?

Alex: You know, Vladimir is a very demanding manager.

Tanja: What does he say about the delay?

Alex: I don't know. Actually, I've been avoiding him, but I'm worried about what he'll say when I see him on Monday.

Tanja: Hm. Let's summarise what we've got so far. Can you do that, please?

Alex: Um, I need two full working days to write 20 to 25 pages, even if I can get the data.

Tanja: OK. So we have the question of making the time. We have the question of how you get the data. And the question of what you say to Vladimir on Monday – you have to talk to him. And the question of writing in English. Right?

Alex: Yes, a lot of questions.

Tanja: But you're good at thinking through this kind of issue. So let's start with the data. How are you going to tackle … ?

Track 17

Interviewer: Sachi, why should we listen to other people?

Sachi: Oh, there are a lot of good reasons for listening.

First of all, we could start with getting information. This is the most obvious reason for listening at work, and people generally do this quite well. Then we can listen to assess competence and trustworthiness. Business people need to make judgements about the people they're dealing with all the time, and listening is part of this. We also want to show other people that we're competent and can be trusted. For example, we may want to convey our own expertise by showing that we understand complex issues. Next, we listen to show respect and build rapport. Taking time to listen to others is an act of respect, and shows your commitment to your relationship with the other person. And another important reason is to understand the speaking style of the person you're talking to, so that your own communication is better with them – thinking about the words they use, how fast they talk, how organised they are ... you may need to adapt your own style to theirs, and listening is important here, too.

Track 18

Interviewer: And what's the return on investment for good listening?

Sachi: There are lots of benefits. Good listening can lead to better relationships at work, more motivated staff, higher productivity, increased creativity, improved quality, fewer mistakes and lower costs, more efficient information flow and happier customers! So everyone gains from better listening.

Interviewer: Are there different kinds of listener?

Sachi: Yes, I think there are three main kinds. People-focused listeners pay a lot of attention to other people's thoughts and feelings. They are patient and ask questions, but may seem unfocused and vague to other kinds of listener. Information-orientated listeners have a more analytical approach to listening – they like to collect and analyse information, in order to understand the situation as fully as possible. Results-orientated listeners, of course, are focused on outcomes, which they want to achieve as quickly and efficiently as possible. They may come over to other kinds of listener as impatient, even pushy and arrogant sometimes.

Track 19

Interviewer: Can we learn to be better listeners?

Sachi: Yes. One way to start is by understanding the learning process. In a brilliant book called *The 7 Habits of Highly Effective People*, Stephen Covey describes five levels of listening: one – ignoring, basically not listening at all; two – pretending to listen; three – selective listening, hearing only parts of what was said; four – attentive listening, paying attention only to the words being said; and five – empathic listening. This kind of listening uses all our senses to understand the speaker's feelings as well as their ideas. In levels one to four, the listener is self-centred. They are busy forming and rehearsing their reply while the other person is speaking. But empathic listening is like hearing with the heart. If you ask yourself what level you're listening at each time you listen, it will help you to listen at a higher level.

UNIT 7

Track 20

John: Oh, yes, good, great job. Well done! Keep up the good work.

Track 21

Elsi: To be absolutely honest, Céline, I was very disappointed. You were vague, you were woolly, you didn't give any facts. I'm really worried about the impression they got of us. You really have to sharpen up your act a bit, you know ...

Track 22

Kenji: Very nice, I thought. I liked your enthusiasm. I think your belief in the project really came across well, especially the second part, when you were talking about expanding into North America. Thanks for doing it.

Track 23

Nick: I thought you did a good job. They got a clear overview of the project, and I think you convinced them about the targets, especially for North America – those came over really well. One thing to work on, though, is getting the balance right between ideas and facts. These financial people want more than just enthusiasm and belief. They're very analytical and they want figures, evidence. I think you should consider adapting your message to fit your audience a bit more. Is that useful?

Céline: Yes, thanks. I'll think about it and work on it for next time.

Track 24

Céline: Do you have a couple of minutes?

Nick: Sure.

Céline: Could you give me some feedback on my presentation?

Nick: OK, but first of all, tell me what *you* thought of it.

Céline: I was reasonably happy. You know I don't like doing presentations, and I still worry that everyone can see how nervous I am. I think I talked too much about the development phase – maybe that was due to nerves as well.

Nick: Well, I thought you did a good job. In fact, I talked about it straight afterwards with the others, and we agreed that it did what it was supposed to do; so thanks from the team for that. And, even if you were nervous, you didn't show it, which is a plus!

Céline: That's nice to hear. Any detailed feedback?

Nick: I thought it was a really strong opening. I liked the first slide – it really got their attention. What I think you could improve on is the way you deal with questions. You need to tell people at the start whether or not you're happy for them to interrupt you. And at the end, when that guy in the front row asked about the research, I think you spent too much time on that, when it wasn't very interesting for everyone else. You could give someone like that a short answer, and then say you'll be happy to talk to them afterwards.

Céline: OK.

Nick: No problem. Was that useful?

Céline: Yes, very helpful.

Nick: You know, I'm doing a big presentation next week to the suppliers' meeting. You can give *me* some feedback on that.

Céline: I'll be happy to.

Track 25

Tomoji: I'm looking forward to the meeting this afternoon. But tell me how you manage meetings here. I think it may be different from Japan. Where will this meeting take place? In the CEO's office?

Monica: No, this one will be in the board room, because there will be quite a lot of people, and it's a big room.

Tomoji: Who can I talk to? Do I have to wait for the CEO to ask me a question?

Monica: No, anyone can talk to anyone. There's no formality in our meetings.

Tomoji: What do people talk about at meetings? Is it business only?

Monica: If you get there a bit early, then you can chat to people before it starts, but once it has started, it's business only until the end. It's not a like a meeting I had in the Gulf once, where it was difficult to know when we were socialising and when the meeting had actually started.

Tomoji: When can you speak?

Monica: You should ask the chair for permission to speak, you shouldn't just interrupt – you can put your hand up. People take turns to speak, and you should wait for the other person to finish before you say anything.

Tomoji: How much can you speak?

Monica: You shouldn't speak for too long. I know in some countries, some senior managers speak for quite a long time and everyone has to listen; but here, you just make your point, and that's it.

Tomoji: And will we really be making decisions during this meeting? Or will everything have been decided beforehand?

Monica: Oh, we will have a real discussion. That's what the meeting is for. It's not just a formality.

Tomoji: Last question. Will it start on time?

Monica: Yes, it should do. And I hope it finishes on time, too!

UNIT 8

Track 26

Dmitri: Hello, Bill. How was your trip to New York?

Bill: Well, I just got back, so I'm feeling rather jet-lagged. What do you want to know?

Dmitri: Actually, I want to know if you have any news about the budget for next year.

Bill: Oh, er, I think this should wait for the next team meeting and then I can make a general announcement.

Dmitri: But can you give us some idea, or can we have a meeting to get your report?

Bill: Why is it so urgent?

Dmitri: Bill, you know we need at least two more engineers on this project. Our new budget is supposed to give us this. We're all really busy, and I'm starting to have problems at home.

Bill: I'm afraid I've been told we can't get two more people on this project. New York just doesn't see how important this project is.

Dmitri: So what's going to happen?

Bill: Listen, I can't just tell you without telling the others. Let's call a meeting for everybody tomorrow morning, and I'll go through the new budget in detail with you all then.

Dmitri: This is very bad. They haven't given us what we need because you were too afraid to ask for it. They know they can walk over you. Nobody knows the fantastic work we're doing here. Most people outside Moscow don't even know we exist! This is not good. I don't want to continue to work like this. I have offers from other banks, you know.

Bill: Dmitri, I know you're great and I know you're doing great work, but it's really difficult to get them to listen. I …

Dmitri: You must make them listen to you. It's not just me. Everybody in the team feels the same. What you have to do is …

Track 27

Isabelle: I'd like to start by welcoming you all to the HR division and to thank you all for taking the time to come here and see our work. It is an honour to have you all here, and I hope you have found the displays of our work informative and interesting. Secondly, I'd like to say a big thank you to our team leader, Marco Lippi, for asking me to make this presentation on behalf of our team. I must admit I'm a bit nervous, but I know everyone is behind me, and I do want to tell you about the great work we've been doing. Not only that – we think there are lessons to be learned from the way that we've managed to achieve and go beyond these targets, which can be applied across the organisation.

Indeed, this is what I want to do – to pick out three particular features of the team's performance to explain to you how we made the regional HR group a driver for change within the organisation. First, I'll describe the way we worked together to achieve this success – since we feel the people side of this and the great team spirit is very important. We spent a lot of time checking things like communication, roles, processes, relationships and so on.

Then I'll briefly describe the more technical side of putting the group in place – which was also quite logistically challenging – and how we tracked progress towards achieving the targets, and also deal with some of the obstacles we met and how we dealt with them. Finally, we have identified some key conclusions about building a regional HR group, which we think are valid for the rest of the organisation and which we would be happy to help promote more widely. So, if that's OK … if there are no questions? … I'll start with the checklist we used to define the objectives and procedures for this project.

Answer key

1 Becoming a better manager

A 4 a A manager is someone who gets results through other people.
b The job of a manager is to lead a team to achieve planned objectives.
c Yes, provided they want to learn.
d The choice between becoming a manager or not
5 a She was very nervous (and quite anxious) about it, because all the people in the team were older than her and had all been in the company much longer and all had their own way of doing things.
b Management By Walking Around
c She learned from her mistakes and she tried to think about what she was doing and to reflect.
6 a manager **b** management **c** managerial **d** manageable
7 a management **b** managing **c** manager **d** managed **e** management **f** management **g** managerial **h** manage
8 1 g **2** h **3** j **4** i **5** f **6** a **7** c **8** b **9** d **10** e
B 2 a The Four Ps are Preparation, Purpose, Process and People.
b Good communication is the key to getting people more involved and getting better results from them.
3 a Preparation **b** Opening **c** Relationship building **d** Structuring **e** Discussing and negotiating **f** Deciding **g** Concluding and summarising **h** Closing **i** Celebrating
4 1 Preparation (statement c)
2 Purpose (statement d)
3 Process (statement a)
4 People (statement b)
5 1 h **2** f **3** a **4** g **5** i **6** b **7** d **8** e **9** c
C 2 a Because more than half of British employees think that they are
b To make good decisions and to communicate with them
c To keep looking forward – to predict potential issues and to prepare for them before they happen
d Schedule a meeting with yourself every week.
4 a rated **b** responds **c** ultimate **d** predict **e** issues **f** scheduling **g** block out **h** headache **i** indicators
5 a Leaders; Managers **b** Leaders; Managers **c** Managers; Leaders **d** Leaders; Managers **e** Leaders; Managers **f** Managers; Leaders **g** Managers; Leaders **h** Managers; Leaders
D 4 a corporate **b** briefing **c** clash **d** shock **e** functional

2 Building a team

A 3 a Getting to know people, and getting people to understand that strong teams thrive on difference
b By using some of the standard team development tools which are available, like the Myers Briggs Type Indicator and the Margerison-McCann Team Management Profile
c Relationships – how you relate to other people at work
Information – how we gather and use it
Decisions – how we make them
Organisation – how we organise ourselves and others
d It helps you to learn to be tolerant of difference.
4 1 Advising **2** Organising **3** Inspecting **4** Innovating **5** Linking **6** Developing **7** Maintaining **8** Promoting **9** Producing
6 a 5 **b** 2 **c** 4 **d** 3 **e** 1
7 a leader **b** lead **c** leading **d** leadership **e** led
B 2 a Using *Frau* or *Herr* (Mr or Mrs)
Using the formal form of *you* in German with each other (*Sie* rather than *du*)
Making a clear distinction between work and life outside work
b Respect
c Younger people are less formal with each other.
d Sometimes she feels uncomfortable, but she quite likes the way things are changing.
3 a A committee of employee representatives from the different European countries where a company is present
b Directly or through interpreters
c Some of the members of the EWC are very informal.
d She thinks a lot of Germans tend to be quite focused on the task, but others may need to know who they're dealing with before they get down to business.
6 a Its activity **b** Your name **c** Your location **d** Your organisation **e** Your job
7 The incorrect phrases are: **1** c **2** b **3** a **4** b
8 1 e **2** g **3** h **4** c **5** a **6** b **7** i **8** f **9** d
C 2 a Where are we going?
b How do we plan to do it?
c Who does what?
d What help is needed?
e How are we seen in the organisation?
f How are we co-operating as a team?
4 a virtually **b** gaps **c** committed **d** matrix **e** ambassadors **f** underpinning **g** synergy **h** model **i** links
5 a 1 **b** 7 **c** 4 **d** 6 **e** 2 **f** 9 **g** 3 **h** 8 **i** 5

3 Getting and giving directions

A 2 a False b False c False d True e True f True
  3 a zones; contractors b Sweden; Denmark
    c public construction project d does not make
    e quite a time f top-down
  5 a process worker b vision c values d intranet
    e directive f Shareholder value g Cascading down
    h boardroom i shop floor

B 3 a To be clear, and to give the right context
    b What do they know about this? What don't they
      know about this? What do they need to know?
    c Direct, serious, careful, organised
    d Keep It Short and Simple; Keep It Simple, Stupid
    e Colleagues who are not organised when they talk
  4 a By helping other people to get the information
      they need so he doesn't have too many people to
      talk to every day
    b Who needs to know this?
    c She prefers phoning and speaking face to face.
      She says that people get too many e-mails.
    d No, she also likes to listen and ask questions.
    e She is informal. She likes to talk and listen. She is
      informal and relaxed. She likes to laugh.
    f She is more serious.
  7 a Formal; Informal b Proactive; Reactive
    c Indirect; Direct d Emotional; Neutral
    e Expansive; Concise f Time-focused; Time-flexible
  8 2 Use simple words.
     3 Be direct.
     4 Speak slowly.
     5 Don't try to be funny.
     6 Avoid local cultural references.
     7 Avoid idiom.
     8 Check and clarify frequently.
     9 Summarise.
    10 Take turns when you speak.

C 3

	quality in order of importance **To be:**	% importance	% of managers seen as competent
1	approachable	83	50
2	a good communicator	82	28
3	supportive	81	38
4	a good leader	80	31
5	respectful of each individual	76	36

  6 a unapproachable b screen-led c struggle with
    d fire off
  7 Leaders: superior, boss, director, executive,
    employer, team leader, supervisor, head, foreman,
    manager
    Followers: report, worker, co-worker, employee,
    wage earner, subordinate, staff member

D 2 a low b high c high d high e low f high
    g low h low i low j high

4 Organising teams

A 4 a Because people need to be clear about their
      objectives *and* how they are going to achieve these
      objectives
    b He says management is getting results from
      people.
    c A couple of hours (between the Friday and the
      Monday meeting)
    d One hour at the Monday meeting
    e Delegation means giving the task to someone else,
      but keeping the responsibility for it.
      Empowerment means someone else taking on the
      task and the responsibility for it as well.
    f Getting people to think and talk more about how
      they work together
  6 a organiser b organised c organisational
    d organise e organisation
  7 a organise b organised c organisational
    d organisation e organiser
  8 a enthusiasm b emotion c explanation
    d engagement e reward f culture g trust
  9

what useless leaders damage	how they do it	how to avoid the same trap
a enthusiasm	micro-management; coercion; disrespect	Try better delegation and informal feedback, plus better, easier appraisal
b emotion	aggression; lack of sensitivity and empathy; poor work–life balance	Publish a personal work-life balance manifesto; develop greater empathy; encourage assertiveness
c explanation	partial, inconsistent communication	Make communication consistent, clear and two-way
d engagement	individual objectives dictated by managers; limited team goals	Allow teams to set their own goals; encourage participation in decision-making
e reward	rewarding the wrong things and offering the wrong sort of rewards (e.g. money for someone not motivated by money)	Give the right rewards to the right people at the right time; establish team rewards; give managers greater flexibility in rewarding staff

f culture	ignoring the difference in cultures during mergers and acquisitions; punishing risk-taking while trying to introduce a culture of innovation	Offer training for managers on influencing culture; allow managers to evolve their own personal mistakes policy
g trust	unfair recruitment or reward decisions	Offer training to managers on procedural justice and fairness; help managers to develop trust in others

B 2 a There is frequently no agenda.
  b 1, 2, 3, 4, 5, 6, 7 are all mentioned.
4 a place **b** time **c** people and roles
  d purpose and content **e** type of meeting
  f facilities **g** documentation
5 a 3 **b** 4 **c** 5 **d** 1 **e** 2 **f** 6 **g** 9 **h** 10 **i** 7 **j** 8

C 2 a Because there is gender bias in assessment processes (selection, promotion and appraisal).
  b It has been 'dominated by US work … based on studies of men, by men'.
  c The heroic model of leadership involves 'notions of larger-than-life, charismatic individuals who excite others to follow them'.
  d '… genuine empowerment – as a partnership, in which the views of the subordinates are taken seriously …'
  e '… the notion that leaders create an environment and relationships which are based on genuine respect, empowerment, collaboration and partnership with their staff, colleagues and other stakeholders, in achieving the organisation's goals.'
  f They are 'more productive, have higher morale and lower stress levels than those that don't'.
4 a contentious **b** patronise **c** susceptible to
  d saviour **e** stakeholder **f** embed **g** rated
  h attributed to
5 a 4 **b** 3 **c** 5 **d** 6 **e** 1 **f** 2

D Case study
1 a Hot-desking in an office occurs when employees do not have their own desks but take whichever desk is free when they arrive at work. The article says *No one at Interpolis has their own fixed work space. The employees can select a place of work that is best suited to them and to the job that they do.*
  b People who have flexible working arrangements have some choice about the times when they start and finish work; and possibly about how far they can work at home as well as on the organisation's premises.
  c Because the company recognises that people need different workspaces to carry out different tasks and also to relax
  d As long as the work gets done
  e Working from home

5 Defining roles

A 2 a The targets are ambitious.
  b Marie in Paris
  c Three
  d 2, 4, 5
5 a launched **b** going over (her) head **c** to pin down
  d matrix (organisation)
6 a for **b** in **c** in **d** under **e** with **f** on
7 a gender roles **b** take on a new role **c** role-play
  d role allocation **e** role model
8 a clarify **b** who; what **c** blurred; ill-defined
  d take; for **e** review; regular
B 2 a 8 **b** 6 **c** 5 **d** 3 **e** 4 **f** 2 **g** 7 **h** 1
5 adjourn, break off, conduct, enter into, renew, resume
6 a outlining **b** purpose **c** items **d** terms
  e alternative **f** willing **g** provided; conditions
7 a 5 **b** 6 **c** 2 **d** 3 **e** 4 **f** 1
8 *Sample answers*
  1 I'm sorry, but can you explain that part again, please?
  2 What exactly do you mean by 'a certain delay'?
  3 Please could you elaborate on the details of the new model?
  4 It's a beautiful part of the city here, isn't it?
  5 Do you agree to these terms?
  6 Could you tell me something about your quality assurance?
C 4 a incentivise **b** subtle **c** assumption **d** intervene
  e implies **f** saviour **g** tactic **h** further **i** agenda
  j phenomenon **k** excuse **l** initiate **m** genuine
6 b Build trust
  c Be transparent
  d Use logical arguments
  e Focus on the relationship
  f Be strong
  g Look to the future
  h Show optimism

6 Providing support

A 4 1 How long will it take me to write the report?
  2 How will I make the time?
  3 How will I get the data?
  4 What will I say to Vladimir on Monday?
  5 How can I deal with the problem of writing the report in English?
5 a issue **b** outcome **c** current situation
  d to get the job done **e** Imagine that
  f would it take then **g** solve **h** summarise
6 a O **b** W **c** G **d** R
7 a R **b** O **c** W **d** G
8 a 4 **b** 5 **c** 4 **d** 1 **e** 2
B 3 a, d, f, h
4 a 4 **b** 8 **c** 5 **d** 6 **e** 7 **f** 9 **g** 2 **h** 1 **i** 3
5 a people-focused **b** information-orientated
  c results-orientated
6 1 Ignoring **2** Pretending **3** Selective **4** Attentive
  5 Empathic
7 a 6 **b** 7 **c** 8 **d** 2 **e** 5 **f** 3 **g** 1 **h** 4

8 a Is this your first time in Tokyo?
  b Do you have a lot of experience of working with Japanese people?
  c It's interesting what you say about Mexican companies.
  d Are you saying that your company will do this?
  e In my experience, it's very important to bear this in mind.
  f Good luck with the project.
C 5 a T **b** F **c** T **d** T **e** F **f** T
  6 a coachee **b** mentee **c** mentee **d** coachee **e** mentee **f** coachee
  8 a reward **b** consult **c** delegate **d** empower **e** mediate **f** arbitrate

7 Giving and receiving feedback

A 2 a a 2 **b** 4 **c** 1 **d** 3
  b negative feedback = being critical of someone's performance, telling someone they have done a bad job
  constructive feedback = giving someone ideas as to how they can improve their performance next time
  praise = telling someone they have done a good job
  positive feedback = telling someone they have done a good job and giving specific reasons for your assessment
  4 a 3 **b** 5 **c** 2 **d** 4/6 **e** 1 **f** 7 **g** 6/4
  5 a Well **b** job **c** efforts **d** helpful **e** appreciate **f** contribution **g** work **h** piece **i** step **j** excellent
  6 a 4 **b** 5 **c** 1 **d** 6 **e** 3 **f** 2
  7 a Accept **b** Take; consider **c** Avoid **d** formulate
B 3 a 1 **b** 1 **c** 1 **d** 1, 3 **e** 3 **f** 2 **g** 1
  6 a arranged **b** get to; chair **c** rescheduled **d** postponed **e** take part **f** cancelling **g** holding
  7 a 4 **b** 6 **c** 5 **d** 2 **e** 3 **f** 1
  8 c 4 **d** 3 **e** 8 **f** 1 **g** 2 **h** 6 **i** 10 **j** 5
C 5 a performance **b** productivity **c** absent **d** lateness **e** standard **f** targets **g** improvement **h** expected
  6

happy	sad	angry	confused
proud thrilled wonderful excited joyful	lonely dissatisfied deflated gloomy fed up miserable	annoyed grumpy irritated furious aggressive hostile	bewildered misunder- stood harassed unclear lost puzzled muddled distraught unsure

8 Representing a team

A 3 a To New York
  b To negotiate a budget for two more engineers
  c No
  d Because he's already overworked
  5 a recognition; demotivated **b** internally **c** overall **d** communication **e** hierarchical; competent **f** ownership **g** visible **h** 'sell' **i** influencing; political
  6 a Influencing **b** Political **c** Technical/Professional **d** Organisational **e** Intercultural **f** Presentation
B 2 *Suggested answers*
  a A fairly senior management group
  b Because the group has come to the team's location to see its work
  c To underline the idea that the work has been a team effort; to give the opportunity to a team member to speak for the team and get experience speaking to more senior people
  d Presenters are usually advised not to admit to being nervous.
  e She uses *we* rather than *I*.
  5 a by heart **b** attention **c** story **d** structure **e** stress **f** main message **g** Vary **h** golden **i** question(er)s **j** yourself
  6 a of all **b** subject **c** aim **d** divided **e** interrupt **f** turn **g** over **h** point **i** recommendation **j** attention
C 2 a T **b** T **c** F **d** F **e** F **f** T **g** T
  4 a out of hours **b** well-being; self-fulfilment **c** business integrity **d** social responsibility **e** business imperative **f** value **g** outstrips **h** resilience **i** psychological contract

Business word combinations

Verb (A–E) + noun
a deal with **b** boost **c** carry out **d** develop **e** establish **f** adopt **g** bring about **h** extend **i** achieve **j** enjoy

Verb (F–J) + noun
a implement **b** fix **c** gain **d** hold **e** focus on **f** increase **g** fail **h** guarantee **i** face **j** handle

Verb (K–O) + noun
a make **b** maintain **c** meet **d** liaise with **e** offer **f** launch **g** obtain **h** manage **i** monitor **j** lead

Verb (P–R) + noun
a resolve **b** reach **c** react to **d** predict **e** raise **f** respect **g** reduce **h** put forward **i** provide **j** run

Verb (S–Z) + noun
a set up **b** take **c** weigh up **d** set **e** sign **f** undertake **g** submit **h** take part in **i** support **j** take up

Word list

Suggested further reading

These are the best books on leadership, management and business communication that I know:

Buckingham, M. and Coffman, C.: *First, Break All the Rules*, 2005, Simon and Schuster Pocket Books

Comfort, J. and Franklin, P.: *The Mindful International Manager*, 2011, Kogan Page

Covey, S.: *The Seven Habits of Highly Effective People*, 2004, Simon and Schuster

Dignen, R. with McMaster, I.: *Communicating Internationally in English*, 2011, York Associates

Kline N.: *Time to Think: Listening to Ignite the Human Mind*, 1999, Cassell Illustrated

Marcus Aurelius: *Meditations*, 170–80, trans. Hammond, M., 2006, Penguin Classics

Nye, J.: *The Powers to Lead*, 2008, Oxford University Press

Townsend, R.: *Up the Organization*, 1970, Alfred A. Knopf

The titles in the Management Pocketbooks series (www.pocketbook.co.uk) are often a useful quick introduction to a wide range of business subjects and skills, both hard and soft.

There are useful ideas, worksheets and materials at www.businessballs.com.

International Management English

International Management English consists of four titles covering key aspects of international business operations: *Leading People*, *Managing Projects*, *Managing Change* and *Working Virtually*. These four titles provide insights into the challenges of working internationally and develop practical skills which will help people to do their jobs more effectively.

Each book in the series consists of eight units, with every unit offering four distinct sections:

- *Discussion and listening* Engaging and relevant content in areas of international management and teamwork.
- *Communication skills* In addition to the familiar topics of meetings, presentations and negotiations, input and practice are also provided in conflict management, team building and giving and receiving feedback.
- *Professional skills* Authentic texts from management writers and thinkers provide the starting point for reflection and discussion among learners.
- *Intercultural competence* A focus on raising cultural awareness followed by an illustrative case study.

Leading People
by Steve Flinders

This helps new and experienced managers to develop leadership skills for working and communicating internationally.

ISBN 978-1-905085-67-5

Managing Projects
by Bob Dignen

This provides practical ideas on how to work and communicate effectively when taking part in or leading international projects.

ISBN 978-1-905085-66-8

Managing Change
by Fiona Mee

This focuses on the communication requirements of those either taking part in or leading business change, including how to handle resistance.

ISBN 978-1-905085-68-2

Working Virtually
by Jackie Black and Jon Dyson

This addresses the communication challenges that global teams face when using information technology to collaborate.

ISBN 978-1-905085-69-9

For full details of this series, please visit the Delta Publishing website:
www.deltapublishing.co.uk